the
WOW!
Workplace

the

WOW!
Workplace

How to build an employee recognition culture
that engages your people and produces big
results for your organization

Mike Byam

Published by The Terryberry Company
2033 Oak Industrial Dr., NE
Grand Rapids, MI 49505
www.terryberry.com

Production supervision and layout design by Jenny Watkins
Cover design and illustrations by Seyferth & Associates, Inc.

ISBN 978-0-615-25299-5

Printed in the United States of America

Acknowledgements

Certainly, due to the subject matter contained within, we want to make sure to recognize and acknowledge the numerous people who have offered ideas, thoughts, concepts, and experiences that have contributed to **The WOW!** **Workplace.** This book represents a real team effort on multiple levels. I wish to give special thanks to:

Tom Nugent
Jenny Watkins
Dave Beemer
Bill Bergstrom
Greg Butterfield
Sarah Reinertsen
Karen Hogan
George Byam
The entire Terryberry Team
The S&A Bunch
All companies and individuals quoted within

Contents

Foreword

Reaching any big goal takes dedication and hard work; the euphoria of success is often equal to the amount of perseverance it took to get there. Or as I say, "The greater the distance, the greater the glory." I have crossed many finish lines, and I have cherished every finisher's medal I earned from each race. We don't often get a medal for our achievements "off the court," but yet the race of life is much longer than any marathon. There are no medals or finishers t-shirts when you reach some of life's personal or work milestones, but why shouldn't there be? These are the moments we must celebrate– the small and big victories along the way. To proudly honor and remember just how far we've come, and just how much further we know we can go. Everyday is an opportunity to celebrate the *WOW!*

Reach higher,
Sarah

Sarah Reinertsen
Ironman Triathlete

Introduction

If you picked up this book, you've probably asked yourself more than once: how can I encourage and motivate (and thus retain) our organization's best people – by helping to build an environment that affirms their unique value and honors their contributions to our shared mission?

You're not alone in your quest. Our research has indicated that business leaders from organizations of all sizes and virtually every sector struggle with this question as they respond to the fast-changing world of the 21st century.

I've spent a fair amount of time thinking about this issue as well. As managing partner of an employee recognition firm, my day-to-day work involves helping organizations all across North America to develop the kind of recognition culture that will serve them best.

At The Terryberry Company, we recently celebrated our 90th anniversary. It was a gratifying time for our team to reflect on our accomplishments over the years in finding ways to develop, implement and manage recognition strategies that work effectively to achieve the organizational goals of our clients and impact employees in a meaningful way.

As we reviewed our history during the past century, we were reminded that Terryberry is in possession of a virtual treasure trove of information and experience on the subject of successful employee recognition programs.

We also realized that, up until now, no one had written the kind of recognition guidebook that could draw from such a huge fund of experience in order to help HR leaders and business people everywhere develop the kind of powerfully effective recognition culture required for organizational success.

Clearly, there was a need for a book of this kind – especially in a world where rapid globalization is triggering frequent changes in the workplace and making it more important than ever to inspire, engage, and retain our talented employees.

As we explored the possibility of taking on the challenge of such a book, we began to interview business and personnel managers all around the country on the subject of employee recognition. Again and again, we asked searching questions about what strategies had worked for these HR leaders, and why.

These conversations powerfully reinforced that there is indeed an effective strategy for enhancing almost any organization by expanding and improving its program of employee recognition.

At Terryberry, our journey in developing recognition initiatives for more than 25,000 clients around the world has led us to give a new name to the key element required for successfully implementing this ground-breaking new approach.

We call it **The *WOW!* Workplace**, and it's simply our light-hearted way of describing what happens when you begin learning how to show your people the kind of authentic, respect-based recognition that will change the way they think about their jobs and their lives.

As a manager who is vitally interested in the well-being of our own people at Terryberry, I've seen "up close and personal" how the incredible power of **The *WOW!* Workplace** can change attitudes and inspire workers to become fully engaged members of a shared enterprise.

I've also participated in numerous, wide-ranging studies over the years that prove one fact beyond any reasonable doubt: building an effective recognition and appreciation program will dramatically impact the positive direction of your organization!

Some Startling Insights...And Lots of Common Sense

As this book will demonstrate again and again, implementing an effective recognition plan can dramatically improve any organization's productivity, along with its financial bottom line. Among the benefits that typically flow from such a program, business leaders and managers will find numerous effects that can be hugely helpful in accomplishing their mission. Such highly positive outcomes frequently include:

- **Enhanced employee retention**
- **Elevated performance and productivity**
- **Increased attendance**
- **Improved safety records**
- **Successful completion of organizational projects**
- **Increased employee engagement**
- **Heightened benchmarks of success – including improved customer service, on-time deliveries and enhanced industry-mandated certification procedures**

As you'll see on page after page, The *WOW!* **Workplace** goes to great lengths to explain how creating or enhancing an effective recognition program usually results in impressive gains on the bottom line.

Proving that such programs are worth their weight in gold is only the start of the process, and readers of this book will discover that most of The *WOW!* **Workplace** is actually devoted to clearly and precisely outlining the steps involved in implementing a powerfully effective recognition strategy.

In this carefully detailed and common sense-based volume, you'll find hundreds of specific "how-to" suggestions and tips designed to take you through the process of building a recognition culture, from start to finish. Among the key topics that are covered (and illustrated with some dramatic stories about employers who got it right – and wrong!), you will find the following:

--- How to listen better, and with more empathy, which is one of the first steps on the road to building a powerful recognition culture.

--- How to put together a formal recognition program by developing memorable awards designed to honor length of service or special achievement, along with staging knockout presentation events guaranteed to evoke a *WOW!* from all recipients.

--- How to build a highly effective informal recognition program that can include everything from surprise, on-the-spot awards for achievement to exciting peer recognition initiatives.

--- How to promote and enhance day-to-day recognition in your organization, whether it comes in the form of a special handwritten note or during a spur-of-the-moment lunch with the division manager or CEO.

--- How to make the moment of recognition unforgettable so that its magical power will make the recipient a loyal, engaged employee for years to come.

--- How to use pinpointed recognition strategies to achieve improved retention of your most talented and dedicated workers.

--- How to target your recognition strategy in order to reach specific goals of improved production and customer satisfaction.

--- How to use recognition principles and techniques in order to motivate better performance from employees who are under-achieving.

Preparing for the Long Run

So what's the key thing you need to know in order to implement a recognition strategy that will work "to the max" for your organization?

In order to answer that important question, I need to bring another one of my passions into the conversation. Over the last ten years I've challenged myself by running marathons and competing in Ironman Triathlons.

Although more than a few of my friends and family members have suggested that I'm a bit nutty to spend so many of my days off consecutively swimming 2.4 miles, biking 112 miles, and then running 26.2 miles, I've found a very useful link between surviving these grueling endurance tests and building a winning recognition strategy within any organization.

The name of that link is: preparation.

Some background: As you might imagine, it didn't take me long to figure out that if I burned up all my energy in the first hour of a five-hour, 100+ mile bike ride (sometimes at 110 degrees and with a desert wind blowing in your face!), I'd soon end up gasping helplessly beside the road and calling for assistance.

What I learned – fast – was that instead of pushing myself into a total meltdown on that bike, I needed to plan every single mile of the journey so that I could remain strong as long as possible and eventually complete the course.

In the same way, I've discovered over the years that the key ingredient for success in building a recognition culture is to plan and prepare so that you can move carefully and effectively through the process, step by step and day by day.

Make no mistake: When it comes to enhancing performance and employee retention with a recognition program, everything depends on the preparation. And if you don't have the proper tools in place before you start, you may very well find success difficult to achieve.

Until now, unfortunately, many of these vital tools have been lacking, both in the workplace and in the executive suites of organizations large and small.

Which is why, after doing lots of in-depth research and conferring with business leaders and HR managers all across North America, I finally decided it was time to write this book.

Based on the latest employee-management and cost-benefit studies from the world of organizational development, **The *WOW!* Workplace** was conceived as a ground-breaking new guidebook for all those who wish to enhance a shared enterprise by establishing an inspiring culture of recognition and appreciation.

Chock-full of detailed instructions and crammed with compelling stories of managers and workers who challenged their attitudes about the value of recognition and thus changed their lives, **The *WOW!* Workplace** will point the way toward a bold new future in which managers and workers alike will benefit by learning how to authentically respect and value each other in ways that seem certain to create a more enjoyable and successful work environment for all!

Mike Byam
Managing Partner, The Terryberry Company

CHAPTER ONE

Understanding the Awesome Power of Employee Recognition

The Bottom Line: Here's why tapping into the amazing power of targeted employee recognition is so important for your organization – and why the best managers routinely include comprehensive recognition initiatives in their leadership approach.

Feed Them and They'll Follow You Anywhere

One summer evening a few years ago, a savvy corporate executive in Michigan staged a brilliant maneuver that would greatly enhance her stature at her manufacturing company - while also helping to assure its future financial success.

The executive's name was Adrienne L. Stevens, and her brilliant maneuver consisted of tossing half a dozen steaks on her backyard grill.

Stevens, the hugely successful president of the $300 million L-3 Avionics Systems in Grand Rapids, Michigan, was about to begin serving dinner to several of her employees.

Wearing a bright green apron and a custom-designed chef's hat marked *SmartDeck®*, Stevens had spent the previous hour pouring cocktails for her delighted guests, all of whom were now lounging contentedly in lawn chairs beside the swimming pool.

The veteran executive managed more than 600 mostly engineering and technical employees located in this country and overseas. As she drifted among her contented visitors, she seemed to be enjoying herself fully. Nodding and smiling, she ambled along beneath a string of softly glowing lanterns at poolside, pausing often to laugh and chit-chat animatedly with the people she was about to feed.

Watching Stevens flip the steaks on her grill a few minutes later, most observers would probably have assumed she was enjoying a night off from her labors as the top executive at L-3 Avionics – a high-flying subsidiary of the giant $13 billion aerospace and defense industry manufacturer, L-3 Communications.

But that assumption would have been wrong. Stevens – a well-seasoned corporate manager who'd climbed the ranks to become one of the very few female aerospace chief executives in her traditionally male-dominated industry – was actually hard at work.

The L-3 Avionics president was engaged in one of the most important tasks that an organizational manager must confront daily: the task of making sure that key employees receive the vital recognition required to win both their loyalty and their maximum creative effort in helping to realize the goals of their organization.

For Stevens, meeting that challenge was especially important since her company was in the middle of an eight-year struggle to design and then begin manufacturing a revolutionary new airplane cockpit instrument control panel (the same *SmartDeck*® system featured on her chef's hat) that had required an investment of more than $100 million.

SmartDeck® had the potential to completely change the instrumentation found on the display panel of the typical Cessna

400 or Piper Cherokee. For the first time ever, in fact, Stevens' company was attempting to completely digitalize and integrate all the instrument components in the cockpit, an engineering innovation that promised to make for much easier (and safer) flight.

SmartDeck® was a thrilling aviation challenge, of course. But for the L-3 engineers and technicians who were involved in the ground-breaking project, it would also prove to be an extraordinarily complex challenge since it required a complete "reinvention" of the basic cockpit instrumentation system that has been standard since the early days of flight.

As the decade-long development phase slowly unfolded, the hundreds of engineers and support staff who were working on *SmartDeck®* had often been forced to revise their blueprints and write millions of brand-new lines of software code in order to meet constantly changing technological demands and manufacturing "specs." For most of these employees, the pace had been grueling and the frustrations had been endless.

For Adrienne Stevens, their fearless leader, the daily task had been how she could bolster the morale and inspire the continuing dedication of her employees. The answer, she soon discovered, was one very simple word.

Recognition.

With the instinct of a born organizational manager, Stevens quickly grasped the central fact on which her entire organization's success would depend.

That simple fact is that the most effective way to motivate employees, improve performance and, as a result, increase any organization's bottom line is to become skilled at using enhanced employee recognition.

As Stevens learned early on, successfully implementing an

employee recognition program (or significantly improving one that's already in place) is worth every dollar and hour you put into it. In 2007, she launched an ambitious and wide-ranging employee recognition strategy known internally as the "WOW Program" which contributed to enhanced productivity at L-3. Indeed, in national survey after national survey (and we'll look at several of them up-close in Chapter Two), the indisputable evidence shows clearly that business leaders and HR administrators who understand the power of employee recognition almost always wind up with a return on investment (ROI) between 200 and 300 percent.

The surveys invariably show – in carefully measured dollars and cents – that for every buck a business manager spends on employee recognition, he or she can realistically expect to get three or four or sometimes even five bucks back.

At L-3 Avionics, the ROI math has always been crystal clear.

Because she was willing to invest generously in recognition programs and strategies for her high-tech engineering talent (including the few dollars spent on that poolside shindig in her own backyard), President Stevens succeeded in keeping up employee morale – even when her company confronted frustrating obstacles that threatened to shut down the entire project.

In the end, says the tireless exec, her investment in employee recognition paid off – handsomely.

These days, Stevens delights in pointing out that *SmartDeck*® is not only into production but has already begun racking up sales orders that now seem likely to earn L-3 Communications gross revenues of more than $100 million each and every year.

While singing the praises of the engineers and L-3 support personnel who made *SmartDeck*® happen, Stevens says, "There's no question that knowing how and when to recognize employee contributions to your organization's mission is absolutely essential. And I also think it's very clear that the ROI for effective employee recognition programs is huge in most cases."

Employee recognition can take many forms. It includes formal recognition programs, where employees are honored for their years of service or their on-the-job achievements. Often tangible, symbolic awards are used to commemorate those special accomplishments. Or it can be informal recognition, like those cookouts Stevens hosts in her backyard, or publicly acknowledging an employee's special effort during a staff meeting.

But whether you stage a formal recognition event or just take the time to tell an employee that you appreciate his or her efforts, there's no doubt that stopping to honor a worker's contribution is absolutely essential to effective management.

A nationally recognized corporate leader with a proven knack for getting the most out of her employees, Stevens says, "I'm convinced that the best recognition you can give anybody is time and attention, along with personal notes. I'm a big fan of handwritten notes and of spending time with people."

Enhanced employee recognition can pay off in a thousand different ways. For one thing, it can allow you to hang onto your best people. And that can literally save you hundreds of thousands of dollars a year; research shows that finding, replacing and then training an employee can easily cost you as much as his or her annual salary. But employee recognition can also improve your company's income statement in many other ways – through increased sales, let's say, or through better quality-control of your products.

Stevens is convinced and says emphatically, "The decision on whether or not to invest some of your time and other resources in an effective employee recognition program is strictly a no-brainer!"

You Don't Need Rocket Science

Like Adrienne Stevens at L-3 Avionics, some of North America's most successful business managers and HR administrators will mince no words in describing the crucial importance of recognizing employees, whether formally or informally.

Their bottom-line message, in exactly 18 words: You don't have to be a Fortune 500 company to understand the value of effective employee recognition programs.

"If my people leave me, I'm done tomorrow," says James Kress, the president and CEO of Voice Data Systems, a thriving, $15 million telecommunications company with about 65 employees.

"Really, you don't have to be a rocket scientist to understand that in a highly technical and complex environment like ours, your employees are, by far, your biggest resource. At VDS, we've invested in several formal recognition programs that provide significant awards to employees for length of service or for special performance achievements of one kind or another.

"But probably the most important thing I do here is walk around the facility and talk to our engineers and technicians," Kress adds. "A lot of it involves praising their work – when they deserve it, of course – and sharing decision-making with them.

"I can tell you that I do my best to be honest and open with every one of my employees," he explains, "because in a very real sense, they're all I have. If I start to lose them, I might as well close the doors because I'll be out of business in a very short time."

As a highly successful manager who implemented a successful strategy that more than doubled the revenue and growth of VDS during a five-year period, James Kress knows exactly what he's talking about. He elaborates on the importance of employee recognition and he points to a stack of information on his cluttered work-desk . . . data that shows, unmistakably, how organizations that ignore employee recognition usually wind up paying heavily for it. As gathered by pollsters like Gallup, Harris and the U.S. Bureau of Labor Statistics, among others, here are just a few of the zingers that tell the lack-of-recognition story in stark, grim detail:

---Organizations with "disengaged" employees who complain that they rarely receive recognition typically experience 50 percent higher turnover rates among their workers than those that use recognition effectively to make employees feel appreciated.

---The productivity rate among organizations with "disengaged" workers is nearly 50 percent lower, on average, than the rate for outfits that emphasize recognition in order to generate appreciation of employees.

---Companies that use employee recognition effectively are 25 percent more profitable, on average, than those that ignore this crucially important aspect of personnel management.

---The cost of replacing neglected employees, who quit their jobs partly because they feel underappreciated, amounts to at least 100 percent of their annual salaries, and often soars to 150 percent.

---More than two-thirds of the employees working for companies without established recognition programs say they feel "no obligation" to remain with their current employers.

The Truck Driver Who Cried

Question: How convincing are these numbers from some of the top workplace pollsters in the country?

Answer: They're plenty convincing, according to some of America's most authoritative management experts.

"Listen, no matter how you slice up the data, the bottom line always comes out the same," says Judith L. Enns, Ph.D., Executive Vice President at HR Solutions, Inc., a major U.S. consulting firm that specializes in helping HR managers to solve workplace problems. "In most situations, employee recognition programs are worth their weight in gold. These programs pay for themselves, in most cases – and they often pay for themselves many times over."

Along with racking up impressive ROI, effective employee recognition programs also serve to build goodwill in both the organizations that sponsor them and the communities where the organizations reside, according to longtime management-employee relations consultant Alex Allion.

"I've spent the past 12 years watching what happens when employees receive awards for their years of service," says Allion, who's based in Scottsdale, Arizona. "This is the formal side of recognition, and I can tell you that getting the formal side right – with appropriate 'exclusive' awards that employees really value, well, that's just critically important for maintaining employee morale and employee motivation.

"A couple of years ago," says the veteran recognition guru, "I was fortunate to be able to attend a farewell banquet at a big national construction company based in San Diego. And the employee was an older truck driver, a tough old guy who was retiring after 25 years on the job.

"Well, as part of my job, I often help the HR folks at that company to design and manufacture custom rings for all their employees. And these beautiful rings are presented at the company's five-, 10-, 15-, 20- and 25-year award celebrations for employees. And the rings are very distinguished with a different number of diamonds in each one, based on the particular employee's years of service.

"This retiring truck driver was a rough-and-tumble, salt-of-the-earth type of guy who didn't say much. But he got up there onstage, wearing blue jeans and a battered old work shirt, and he was presented with this custom ring that had five diamonds in it. And you know what? He teared right up. It was very emotional. Here was this great big guy, this burly truck driver, and he hugged the owner of the company. He just stepped away from the microphone and hugged him. And all the people got up on their feet. It was a jam-packed event, and suddenly we were all caught up in a standing ovation."

Allion says, "I'm telling you, I got goose bumps and I know I'll never forget that moment. What we were witnessing that night was a real force of energy, a real power. It was the power of recognition!"

*In Chapter Two, we'll see how using the power of recognition to create a **WOW! Workplace** for your organization can pay some very real dividends.*

Employee Recognition: 10 Quick Tips

What's the best way to quickly begin enhancing your employee recognition program without having to spend a lot of money or turning your organization's employee management system upside down?

In an effort to answer that question, we talked with hundreds of HR managers and business executives all across North America.

Their many years of experience with recognition strategies taught us a crucially important lesson; to get it right, you have to think about recognizing your employees, and you have to be creative about both formal and informal recognition.

To get you started, here are ten quick tips for powerfully effective recognition, derived from hundreds of hours of interviews and dialog with employers.

First things first. When a new employee arrives on the scene, take a few minutes to drop by the newcomer's desk and say hello. Explain that you're very interested in seeing the new arrival do well on the job, and that you'll be checking in from time to time to see if you can help with the adjustment process. "Most employees vividly remember their first few days on a new job," says Nora Swart, Vice President for Human Resources and Training at the Lake Michigan Credit Union. "If you're there for them on day one with a warm smile of welcome and lots of support, they'll form a bond with you that can last for years. This is a good example of informal recognition at its best." Remember, you never get a second chance to make a first impression.

What's in a name? Everything! As the managing partner at Terryberry, I make it my business to learn the names of each and every one of our team members. As a manager, I'm convinced that purposeful employee recognition starts with learning the names of the folks who are working for you – wherever and whenever that's feasible.

Feed 'em and they'll follow you anywhere. Want to really reward a few of your best workers for a job well done? The way to a worker's heart is through the stomach. Like the backyard barbeques that Adrienne Stevens hosts for her dedicated L-3 engineers, sharing a meal can be a great motivational tool. "Over the years," says Stevens, "I've discovered that when you invite people into your home and cook for them, something magical happens. They realize: 'She's doing this for me, herself; that's how much she cares.' And they never forget that meal." Whether you bring your team to your home for a bite, or chow down on pizza together in the conference room, it's important to remember to kick off the meal by thanking your guests for their extra effort and the impact it makes on the group's success that led to this celebration.

Find recognition awards that "just keep on giving." To get maximum bang for your employee-recognition buck, use awards that will impact your honoree today, tomorrow and six months from now. Remember that symbolism is what makes an award memorable, so choose an item that makes a statement about what the individual accomplished. Consider engraving the achievement date on the award or tying in your corporate symbol. Awards that are displayed or used frequently will trigger positive thoughts about the recognition experience time and again.

Score a hit on the home front. In today's fast-moving and high-tech workplace, there are no louder buzz words than "work-life balance." So how can you address that key issue when recognizing an employee's job performance? It's simple. Let's say a group of your employees worked tons of overtime (including late nights and weekends) getting that last big project out the door. Then one afternoon, a few hours before their mealtime, their home doorbells ring and when they open the door, the delivery person says, "Dinner is served!" While they feast on the goodies from a local gourmet deli, they're reading your handwritten recognition note, "Since you put in so much extra time at work, I wanted to save you some time in the kitchen."

Embrace pomp and circumstance. An occasion to present public recognition is an opportunity to really *WOW!* a deserving employee, so let's do it up right! Put out a great spread, queue the lights, and roll the slideshow. And above all else, put some careful thought into the words that are spoken about the recipient. What employees will notice – and remember permanently – is which company executives made an appearance and what they said. Former Benefits Manager at BMW of North America, Wendy Jacob adds, "Making sure that the award recipient's boss is on hand isn't enough; you should also try to make sure that the boss' boss attends and says a few words. And they should be carefully selected words about the specific contributions that the employee made to the company. Those two things – the people and the words that get spoken – are absolutely essential to getting the award presentation right."

Put words of praise on paper – and then put 'em in the mail. What's the best way to recognize an employee who's made a truly outstanding contribution to your organization's mission? For maximum recognition firepower, get the president or director or CEO of your outfit to handwrite a personal note of praise on some high-quality stationery, and then mail the missive directly to the employee's home. In most cases, you can rest assured that this personal note from the top executive will occupy a place of honor on display in the recipient's home.

Buy everybody a hot fudge sundae in the name of your honoree. Want to make that dedicated overachiever feel like a million bucks but spend a whole lot less? Just print up some nifty-looking coupons that say something like: GOOD FOR ONE FREE HOT FUDGE SUNDAE at the nearest old-fashioned ice cream parlor. Near the bottom of the coupon, include a brief message explaining that this free treat is in honor of the employee who's being recognized and that his or her outstanding contribution is the inspiration for today's ice cream freebie.

Add punch and pizzazz to business cards by making them tools of recognition. Did your highly esteemed employee recently win a sales award? Is he or she celebrating 10 or 15 years with your organization? If so, why not tell the world all about it by creating a fancy logo or gold-embossed title that will appear on the honoree's business card along with the usual information? Who wouldn't like to hand somebody a business card that reads something like this?

John Q. Citizen, Sales
ABC Corporation
--Midwest Golden Circle Award Winner

When times are tough and budgets are tight, expand your recognition program instead of cutting it back. This may be the single most important tip to be found in this book because it makes an absolutely crucial point; employee recognition isn't a luxury and it isn't a program you can safely slash every time you want to save a few bucks. On the contrary, recognizing the value of employees is an essential part of success in any enterprise and if you simply understand that one key fact, you're already halfway down the road toward building the kind of employee recognition program that will pay for itself over and over again.

CHAPTER TWO

Employee Recognition and ROI
The Numbers Tell the Story

The Bottom Line: Implementing or significantly expanding an effective employee recognition initiative will earn your organization, on average, a 200 to 300 percent return on investment (ROI).

The "Chief HR Knowledge Officer" Tells It Like It Is

It was Sunday afternoon in the Windy City, and the world's largest organization of human resource professionals was about to launch a gigantic get-together known as the SHRM Annual Conference & Exposition.

From all around the globe, more than 13,500 members of the Society for Human Resource Management (SHRM) were hurrying toward an enormous arena – Chicago's famed McCormick Place Convention Center, a football-stadium-sized showplace that contains nearly two million square feet of exhibition space. While more than 700 exhibitors worked to hammer together the gaudy display booths and neon-flashing product advertisements that would provide the backdrop for the conference, a moment of drama was taking place in a press room on the fifth floor.

Here – in a crowd of bustling reporters and television cameras – one of the world's most knowledgeable experts on HR was about to announce her latest findings.

The information that Debra J. Cohen Ph.D., SPHR, was about to release would be avidly reviewed in the days ahead by HR professionals looking for the very latest industry trends.

As the "Chief Knowledge Officer" of the 245,000-member SHRM, Dr. Cohen directs daily affairs at the organization's Knowledge Center. A nationally recognized expert on HR trends and demographics, she is widely regarded as the SHRM research guru. Given Dr. Cohen's status in the world of HR, it was easy to understand the excitement at the jam-packed SHRM news conference as she ticked off her latest findings on such topics as minority hiring, compensation and benefits, and HR management best practices. For more than an hour, the HR guru did her best to update everyone present on the latest trends in employee management.

And there was also time to ask the Chief Knowledge Officer a question that hadn't yet been asked. A reporter spoke up:

Q. Dr. Cohen, some surveys from recent years have shown that building an effective employee recognition program will usually pay off on an organization's bottom line. According to the latest research at SHRM, do you believe that statement is accurate?

A thoughtful, no-nonsense scientist who had spent 10 years as a professor of human resource management at the George Washington University before joining SHRM, Dr. Cohen answered, "In recent years, there have been many different surveys on the bottom-line value of recognizing employees for their time in service or their contributions at work and the results have usually been the same.

"At this point, I don't think there's any doubt that such programs – provided they are effectively implemented and managed – can help to retain key employees and also increase productivity. The data seems to make that pretty clear. There has also been a lot of scholarly research in this area during recent decades.

"Studies show that HR leaders who do a good job of recognizing their employees can usually expect a significant return on investment."

Describing the surveys, Dr. Cohen pointed to findings from numerous research firms in recent years that showed the ROI for effective employee recognition often averages nearly 300 percent.

Then, with a thoughtful smile, she added, "I think this is one area of research where the issue isn't in doubt. Effective recognition programs are usually a wise investment, and organizations that manage them well are going to benefit in a lot of different ways – and especially on the bottom line."

Investing in Recognition: A Total Slam-Dunk

So how convincing is the research data on ROI for employee recognition programs when you really start to eyeball it up close?

According to the highly regarded trend researchers who put together the recent authoritative *WorldatWork Survey Report: Trends in Employee Recognition*, the return on investment among more than 4,600 organizations actually averaged slightly higher than 300 percent.

The WorldatWork Survey leaves little doubt about the value of building employee appreciation programs as a way of enhancing financial results. Says Terryberry's National Sales Manager, Bill Bergstrom (an award-winning employee recognition expert who consults frequently with some of North America's top corporations): "If you look at the latest studies, they all show clearly that these programs will pay for themselves many times over in only a few years. Every time I show a client one of the ROI surveys, I realize all over again that the decision to invest in employee recognition isn't just sensible – it's a total slam-dunk."

The huge WorldatWork study also clarified some other important issues related to employee recognition practices and their impact on organizations. Among the more interesting findings from WorldatWork were the following:

---More than 89 percent of U.S. companies today use recognition programs as part of their human resources strategy – up from 84 percent just a few years ago.

---The most frequently used recognition programs include various kinds of symbolic gifts, awards, certificates, or other honorifics to salute employees for:

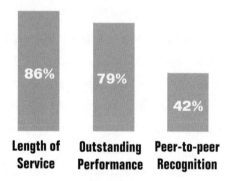

---When listing the reasons for choosing to implement or expand an employee recognition program, the polled organizations ranked their objectives as follows:

Create a positive work environment	77%
Motivate high performance	71%
Create a culture of recognition	69%

While assessing the bottom-line significance of the survey, WorldatWork Recognition Practice Leader Alison Avalos made it clear that using effective recognition strategies is a cost-effective way to build morale in the fast-moving global marketplace. "In the current tug-of-war between workers' demands for higher wages to pay for higher living costs and companies looking to cut costs," said Avalos, "recognition programs can play a key role in creating a positive environment. As such, we expect budgets for recognition programs – currently at 2.7 percent of payroll – to rise steadily. Employee recognition will continue to be a critical component of an organization's total rewards toolkit."

Jerry Lemonds' Night To Remember

If you want to understand the psychological power that can be generated by a well-run recognition program, you should talk to a Maryland gentleman by the name of James G. ("Jerry") Lemonds.

He loves to talk about the night his employer honored him and gave him a special citation to celebrate his 10 years of government service, service that was also honored with the award of a spiffy new fishing rod and reel and a leather-bound Book of Friendship that contained personal notes signed by 100 of the employees he had managed.

"After the roasting, I stood there at the microphone and did my best not to cry," says Lemonds, who later enjoyed reflecting on the magical moment when his supervisors at the Maryland Workers' Compensation Commission saluted him for his decade of loyal service at the agency.

For the grateful Lemonds, the former deputy director of the Commission, the glittering length-of-service award was "a beautiful symbol" of the affection and the respect his agency was displaying for him on that unforgettable evening.

"Receiving that award made me feel marvelous," Lemonds recalls today. "I had my oldest son, Joe, with me that night, and it was a wonderful thing to share that moment with him. When you work for an outfit that cares enough about you to put together an event like that, you wind up feeling very loyal and very motivated. As a state administrator in two state governments, I long ago became convinced that these recognition awards are extremely important when it comes to making the members of an organization feel valued and appreciated."

Describing how effective recognition of employees made him a better manager during his 30 years of government service, Jerry Lemonds loves to point out that he was able to reduce turnover by 20 percent and absenteeism by 40 percent during one particular nine-year period in which he kept careful records. "We later estimated that these retention and absenteeism gains – the result of recognizing and rewarding our workers in ways that really mattered – resulted in cost savings of more than $104,000. That's a huge payoff from recognizing employees."

Adds Lemonds, after describing the giant bass he later caught with his new fishing gear, "What's important here isn't the engraved piece of silver or the personalized watch they give you after so many years on the job. The physical awards are nice and they're important, but they're only symbols.

"What really matters is what those symbols stand for, which is the recognition you got for your efforts as a member of the organization where you spent all those hard-working years. The experience leaves you with a *WOW!* that you remember forever."

As Jerry's story demonstrates, using recognition to build a **WOW! Workplace** can create a powerful sense of loyalty and motivation. But what happens if you don't get it right and wind up trying to manage an organization with employees who feel ignored and unappreciated? In the next chapter, we'll take an up-close look at some nightmarish situations in which the lack of recognition helped to trigger organizational disasters.

Recognition: A Key To Retaining Top Talent?

True or false: When valued employees suddenly decide to pull up stakes and move on to another job, the root cause is, most frequently, a lack of compensation.

You may be surprised to learn that this statement is actually *false*.

Workers all across North America are far more likely to say sayonara over the lack of recognition for their contributions than over paychecks that seem too small.

Hard to believe? Maybe – but it's true. As the managing partner at one of North America's most established employee recognition firms, I've talked with hundreds of employers about this issue, and the vast majority agree that when workers head for the door, it's most often because they feel painfully ignored.

That's also the conclusion that was reached by the U.S. Department of Labor (later reported in *Forbes* magazine) which showed that more than 64 percent of workers leave their jobs, not because they want more money, but because they don't feel appreciated.

In fact, Heritage Medical Associates, PC in Nashville Tennessee found effective recognition to be a key factor that allowed them to cut their turnover rate by more than half. As a part of a strategic plan to improve retention, the management began recognizing employees for their tenure. Three years after implementing their service recognition program, *MGMA Connexion* reported that Heritage Medical Associates' turnover rate had been cut by more than half - from 50 percent to just 20 percent.

Annual Turnover Rate

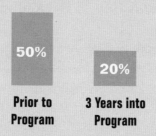

50%
Prior to Program

20%
3 Years into Program

The take-home message here is that taking the time to recognize and applaud employees isn't just about being "thoughtful and considerate" toward your talented, valuable workers. It's about keeping those talented, valuable workers with your organization.

It's actually about your bottom line – which means that it's about success vs. failure – and even about organizational survival.

Get it wrong, and sooner or later your company or organization will wind up paying the price.

Get it right, though, and you'll build a culture in which your best people desire to stay and contribute.

CHAPTER THREE

Without Employee Recognition, Everything That Can Go Bad...Will!

The Bottom Line: Organizations that fail to develop effective employee recognition strategies will pay for it many times over – often with increased turnover rates, deteriorating customer service, and reduced productivity. In addition, unrecognized employees who feel little loyalty toward their organizations won't feel obligated to alert managers to potentially damaging problems or take care of customers.

A Nightmare in Chicago

If you're like most airline passengers these days, you've probably experienced your share of air travel horror stories – nightmarish mess-ups that leave exhausted travelers stranded all day or searching desperately for their lost baggage. Threats of terrorism and the soaring cost of petroleum-based jet fuel have put enormous pressure on the airline industry, and these horror stories of delayed flights and dismal service regularly make the front page of the newspaper and the nightly network news.

Many of these stories are unnerving, to say the least. But for sheer aggravation and gut-wrenching infuriation, it would be hard to match what happened to a close friend of mine at Chicago's famously overcrowded O'Hare Airport. For my friend Tom, a veteran magazine writer and airline passenger who flies around the country frequently to cover stories, the nightmare began around midnight on a freezing winter night when he hurried up to a Chicago departure gate for a flight home that was due to leave in about 20 minutes.

After scurrying through the terminal for nearly half a mile in order to make his connection, Tom was understandably relieved to find that he still had plenty of time to board his plane, which was sitting right there in front of him on the other side of the giant windows at the departure gate.

But there was a problem.

Although the schedule board beside the gate showed that Tom's flight wouldn't be leaving for more than 18 minutes, the departure lounge was deserted and the gate was locked. With growing uneasiness, Tom watched the minutes tick away. There was his airplane only 20 yards away. Why wouldn't they open the gate and let him board?

With only ten minutes left before the scheduled takeoff, Tom grabbed his bags and sprinted back down the concourse to the only other gate where an airline employee was working at this late hour. "Can you please help me?" he called to a yawning attendant. "I'm supposed to be on Flight 124 at Gate 22. Here's my ticket, and the plane is sitting right there. But the gate is locked and there's nobody around."

Shrugging indifferently, the attendant picked up the phone and dialed a few numbers. But he got nowhere, and finally told Tom, "All I can tell you is that the plane won't depart for a few more minutes.

You better run back to the gate and try to get on-board."

Truly alarmed now – since there would be no more planes out of Chicago that night that were headed for his destination – Tom scrambled frantically back down the concourse and pounded on the gate. Nothing. Another two minutes passed. The plane was still sitting there.

And then, suddenly, the door opened and the gate attendant, seeing Tom's panicked look, quickly said, "I'm sorry, sir, but we've closed the door of the plane. No other passengers will be permitted to board."

Amazed, Tom waved his boarding pass. "But I have a ticket that guarantees me a seat on that plane, and there are still five minutes before it's scheduled to depart."

The attendant refused to look him straight in the eye. "I'm sorry, sir, the door is locked and there's nothing I can do."

With that, she picked up a clipboard from the reception desk and marched away out of sight.

It dawned on Tom immediately – even though his flight was still parked right there in front of him – that he would have to spend the entire night in the airport, sleeping on a bench before catching the next flight home at 8 the next morning.

But the story doesn't end there. Because he's a reporter (and because he now had nothing else to do), he decided to try and find out exactly why the airline had decided to ignore its own passenger and his perfectly valid ticket.

Within a matter of minutes, Tom was interviewing half a dozen bored, late-shift attendants, all of whom were telling him the same basic story.

"They keep telling us we're lucky to even have a job," said one resentful clerk after another, "and they could care less about what we think or how we feel. We're being ignored and that makes it very easy to ignore our customers."

When employees aren't recognized or valued by their employers, it won't be long before everything that can go bad does. At the deeply troubled airline, that sad story has been told again and again by outraged passengers who couldn't believe that customer service had become this bad.

The Unseen Problem: Lack of Recognition

In the annals of poorly managed employee relations, the problems at the struggling Chicago airline clearly rank near the top of the list. But the troubled airline hardly stands alone among organizations that have been forced to learn – the hard way – that failing to build a culture of recognition often carries a very high price.

How widespread is the problem? While researching this question and interviewing organizational leaders far and wide, I found many examples of situations in which a lack of effective employee recognition resulted in painful setbacks for management. The purpose here isn't to put down the organizations that have made mistakes in this key area of employee relations; it's simply to help organizations avoid making these missteps. Some harrowing instances:

At a recent employee awards banquet staged at a mid-size construction company (about 200 employees) near Cincinnati, the CEO took the microphone to praise a 10-year-veteran welder for his "outstanding contribution to our mission as one of the premier homebuilders in the Midwest." The CEO went on to praise the welder to the skies. But the effect on the audience was considerably marred when the CEO continually mispronounced the employee's Czech-American name from the beginning of his remarks to the end.

Dreadfully embarrassed, the mortified welder and his family and friends kept their eyes on the carpet throughout the salute.

Says national recognition expert John Bergstrom while describing the impact of such recognition disasters, "When you're putting together an awards program for employees, you have to think your way carefully through the entire presentation and even take some careful notes if you think you need them.

"When it comes to awards presentations, you run a real risk of creating a de-motivating scenario that will actually harm organizational morale if you don't get it right. This is why it's so important to understand the essentials of employee recognition."

One morning a few years ago, a small-town newspaper copy editor in Florida arrived at the paper to begin her first day of work. After greeting her boss and a few colleagues, the newcomer proceeded to the employee break-room where a fresh pot of coffee was there for the taking. She grabbed one of the cups sitting by the pot, filled it to the brim and carried it back to her new work area.

Imagine her horror a few minutes later when the newspaper publisher appeared in her doorway. Glaring with irritation, he bluntly informed her, "That's my cup" before storming off.

Instead of welcoming the new arrival to her first day of work – an absolutely essential requirement for effective employee recognition – the insensitive publisher had destroyed her morale for keeps. In doing so, he revealed that he was completely out of touch with the widespread practice of "on-boarding," which finds business leaders going to extraordinary lengths to make sure newly hired workers are made to feel welcome and valued, starting on day one.

As you might expect, the publisher's behavior was a symptom of problems throughout the newspaper. The wounded copy editor soon left her position at the Florida paper, but years later, she would still remember every detail from that awful morning. "First impressions are lasting," she said, smiling. "I was forever going to be known as the ditz who stole the publisher's treasured coffee mug. I'm glad I'm out of there."

When the sales force at a mid-size office supply company (about 100 employees) in the Atlanta area gathered for its yearly awards banquet, spirits were running high. But then the company CEO got up to salute each and every member of his outstanding team as he presented each with gift cards for meals at local restaurants. Perplexed, the recipients stared at each other. Apparently, the man at the microphone didn't know his team very well. He didn't seem to understand that these hard-charging company reps spent half their lives out on the road, selling their products. They ate out every other night, and the last thing they wanted was to spend a precious night sitting in a restaurant when they could be at home.

Recognition Failure: Here's Why It's So Harmful

Getting it wrong can have a huge negative effect on attitudes in the workplace. "There's no doubt that failing to acknowledge and recognize employees often leaves them feeling disengaged from their jobs," says longtime Gallup Organization researcher James Harter.

"Research also shows that such feelings of disengagement contribute heavily to absenteeism and lower productivity," adds Harter, "along with turnover rates that are 31-51 percent higher than those for business units with engaged employees."

Graig King, a veteran employee recognition counselor in Mississauga, Ontario, says he couldn't agree more with Harter. Adds King, "I think it's very important to understand that recognition is one of the least costly investments in your employees, yet it makes a huge impact. Let's put it in perspective. Relative to efforts like training or ongoing education or movement within a corporation, recognition is usually going to bring you significant ROI at a much smaller out-of-pocket expense."

Concludes the thoughtful advisor, summing up a decade of research on employee-management relations, "Because employee recognition is such a powerful and valuable tool for employers, messing it up by failing to understand the essentials of building a recognition culture isn't just a mistake, it's an absolute disaster."

Recognition Myths: The Top Five

What's the biggest obstacle on the road to building a powerfully effective employee recognition strategy for your organization?

Dave Beemer, a recognition expert and Partner in the Terryberry Company, says that the most common roadblock is making false assumptions. "When it comes to recognizing employees and letting them know you value their services, business people often leap to assumptions that are based on nothing more than myth," says Beemer.

So what are some of the most common myths about recognizing employees that still exist today?

Myth No. 1: If I go out of my way to recognize and reward employees, they'll think I'm a "softie," and the next thing I know they'll start trying to take advantage of me.

Fact behind the myth: Research consistently demonstrates the opposite. Employees who are authentically recognized and valued for their contributions tend to feel more respect for their supervisors, not less. That respect motivates them to work much harder to achieve the organization's goals.

Myth No. 2: All employees really care about is money; give 'em a nice bonus at the end of the year and they'll be yours forever.

Fact behind the myth: Interviews with thousands of employees in recent years prove conclusively that most prefer thoughtful, uniquely individual recognition gifts and acknowledgments to cash, which is simply regarded as additional income.

Myth No. 3: This is a competitive business, and we can't afford to waste precious time and money on recognition awards and ceremonies.

Fact behind the myth: Nothing could be further from the truth. These days, there's overwhelming evidence to support the fact that effective recognition programs and strategies pay for themselves many times over – in reduced employee turnover and increased productivity.

Myth No. 4: I expect our employees to do a good job day in and day out, so recognizing them for doing the job they were hired to do is a waste of time.

Fact behind the myth: Sure, you have every right to expect high standards of performance from your workers.

But even a high-performing employee is capable of reaching for that little extra – if you provide the motivation. All those little extras can add up to huge productivity gains for your organization.

Myth No. 5: Employee X gets too much recognition already, and more praise will spoil her.

Fact behind the myth: Sorry, but the psychologists all say there's no such thing as too much recognition. According to the brain scientists, high achievers are that way precisely because they can never get enough recognition; the more you give them, the harder they'll work at trying to help accomplish your organizational mission.

CHAPTER FOUR

First Step in Building a Powerful Recognition Culture: Learn To Listen!

The Bottom Line: Knowing how to listen to employees is absolutely essential for building the kind of recognition culture that will quickly begin to improve your organization's bottom line. But listening effectively isn't as simple as it looks. Here's why being a good listener matters so much and how to start getting better at it today.

Art Fry's Amazing Eureka! Moment

How important is it for business people to listen to their employees?

A gentleman named Art Fry, a nationally recognized inventor and product developer, might answer that question by describing his amazing adventure as the developer of one of the most successful business products in recent history.

"What happened to me at 3M is a remarkable story," the now-retired chemical engineer has often told reporters. But then he goes on to point out that it certainly wouldn't have happened if his boss hadn't been willing to listen to him and if his company hadn't recognized and respected its employees.

Fry's odyssey began back in the mid-1970s in a rather unlikely setting, the choir loft of North Presbyterian Church in St. Paul, Minnesota.

During Sunday morning services on that fateful day, Fry opened his hymnal and watched a slip of paper marking the page drop out and flutter to the floor.

Irritated that the bookmark had escaped from his grasp, the 3M chemical engineer frowned and leaned down to retrieve the elusive page-finder. It was at this moment that his eyes lit up with a sudden inspiration.

Wait a minute, the product-development researcher told himself. What if we put some of that new "weak adhesive" on the back of my bookmark? Wouldn't that keep it in place without damaging the hymnal?

Fry wanted to shout, *Eureka!* Excited and eager, he couldn't wait to begin tinkering with his new concept.

Although he didn't realize it at the time, Fry had just taken the first step in creating a brand-new, $1 billion a year product that would eventually take the world by storm, a product called Post-it® Notes.

Within the next few years, this simple-sounding innovation – a paper slip coated with "weak adhesive" that could be easily attached to any paper surface and then pulled away without tearing or even wrinkling the material beneath it – would become one of the greatest product success stories ever.

But it almost didn't happen.

When Fry took his new not-so-sticky-notes to 3M's product-development executives, they were not impressed. Nobody's going to buy a bunch of pieces of scrap paper with some weak glue on them, they said.

But wait. Fry's immediate boss – a thoughtful, open-minded product-development supervisor named Robert Molenda – decided to listen to his employee, obeying an important commandment of effective employee recognition: Honor thy employee's words and pay close heed to his or her insights about the workplace.

During the next few years, Molenda not only encouraged Fry to continue his research, but he also approved several funding requests that permitted the never-say-die engineer to work on the project in his own basement.

The results are the stuff of legend. It would take six years of Fry's hard work and Molenda's listening and believing before Post-It® Notes would be introduced across the United States in 1980. Today, the Post-It® Brand is as identifiable as Microsoft Windows® or the McDonald's Big Mac®, and the concept has morphed into more than 600 different products that are sold in 100 countries around the world.

Take heed. It would never have happened if Fry's boss hadn't been smart enough to listen to him.

Wait – The Janitor Has a Better Idea

Knowing how to listen to your employees is an absolutely crucial part of managing any organization effectively. And successful business people will tell you that developing effective listening skills is also a vital ingredient in building the kind of recognition culture required for success. If you think about it, listening is, in itself, a form of recognition; it's an extremely powerful way of telling workers that your organization cares deeply about their creative insights and ideas, and it also conveys that the organization will go out of its way to acknowledge and reward employees who provide insights and ideas.

Nationally recognized management counselor Dwight Peters,

who has spent the past 25 years helping organizations to create powerfully effective employee recognition programs all around the world says, "Obviously, you can't be a good manager unless you know how to listen, and study after study shows that paying attention to what workers tell you will often pay huge dividends."

Several recent business scenarios provide examples in which listening carefully to employees paid off big time.

At Stanford University in California, supervisors at the school's physical plant were smart enough to listen to a truck driver who pointed out that many of the dozens of giant trash receptacles scattered around the campus were less than half full when trash trucks came by to empty them. Based on the thoughtful driver's suggestion, planners at the university were able to switch to smaller dumpsters that could be emptied less frequently. The school began saving more than $150,000 a year that had previously been spent on needless trash pickups.

At a mid-size ($16 million a year) manufacturer of cosmetic supplies in St. Louis, a creative employee questioned the company's practice of shredding and then dumping hundreds of tons of wastepaper each year. Her terrific suggestion was to use the shredded paper as packing material for all shipments leaving the factory. Not only did her idea help the planet by reducing waste, the cosmetics outfit immediately began saving more than $130,000 per year on packing materials.

At the famed Cortez Hotel in San Diego, planners decided to build a new elevator at the center of the huge facility. And when a longtime hotel janitor complained that tearing a hole in every floor would create "a huge mess," they didn't just scoff and tell him to go back to mopping and sweeping. Instead, they listened and asked, "OK, do you have a better idea?" The janitor did, and the hotel installed an exterior glass elevator that saved more than $1 million in construction costs. But the best part is that the elevator became a famous area landmark, helping to bring more guests through the doors.

"It's really amazing," Peters says of the simple concept of listening, "how many great innovations have come from employees who had brilliant suggestions. There's no doubt that any organization can benefit from the thoughts and ideas generated by loyal employees – provided that you are wise enough to listen to them."

Don't Miss A Great Idea...Learn To Listen!

If you're like most business people today, you already understand the vital importance of listening to employees when they talk about the complex workplace challenges they face each day. Developing "leaders who listen" is a key to creating a *WOW!* **Workplace** where employees will be willing to share their ideas.

But did you know that listening effectively to others doesn't really come naturally, that it requires discipline and creativity – and that you can get better at it with some practice?

It's a proven fact. Here are 10 steps you can take to become a better listener.

One: Ask! You'd be amazed how many managers miss this seemingly obvious step. But when you ask for input and show your people that you have a sincere interest in their thoughts, you'll find an untold wealth of brilliant ideas and solutions to problems you may not even have known existed.

Two: Prepare to listen. Schedule periodic meetings with your people to sit down and just "hear them." Ask each employee to bring two or three challenges or opportunities they've noticed and a possible solution to each. Before sitting down, review the topics to be discussed and make sure you have appropriate reference materials (files, correspondence, Web site addresses, etc.) at your fingertips.

Three: Clear your mind. Even tentative employees open up when they know their managers will hear them with thoughtfulness and respect. To give your undivided attention, remove all distractions from your desk or other listening space. Silence your phone, hibernate your computer and put your other work aside. Ask yourself if you are really ready to listen.

Four: Focus, focus, focus. As your conversation begins, look your employee in the eye and keep your gaze focused there. Don't let it wander to the clock on the wall or elsewhere. As you listen, keep asking yourself, "What am I hearing, and what does it tell me about this person and their work?"

Five: Button it! Ever heard that old Irish saying? "God gave us two ears but only one mouth – which means we're supposed to listen twice as much as we talk." Any management consultant will quickly tell you, "biting your tongue" in order to concentrate on what you're hearing is one of the keys to being a good listener. Scribble down any questions or suggestions you might have for later and keep your trap shut until the time is right to speak.

Six: Don't ask "dead-end questions." When the proper time comes to ask questions, focus them on how and why rather than posing yes-or-no queries that will shut down the dialogue. Example: If an employee complains about a problem, don't ask, "Are you upset about that?" Ask instead, "Can you tell me how that problem affects you and your work?" Knowing how to frame questions is an important part of listening well.

Seven: Redirect respectfully. From time to time, it can be necessary to channel an associate's creative energy in a different direction. Here's a three-part method for how to do this without stifling your innovator's desire to share future ideas. 1) Acknowledge the idea. 2) Praise a positive aspect, then 3) Avoid the word "but" (use "and" instead) and invite the individual to contribute in a more beneficial way.

Eight: Paraphrase what you're hearing. From time to time, repeat what the employee is saying (but in slightly different words) to show you understand the key points being made. You'll be surprised how often this technique lets you uncover misunderstandings about what's actually being said.

Nine: Take brief but accurate notes. It's a surprising fact but most of us have forgotten 50 percent of every conversation by the time it ends, according to psychologists. And within 48 hours, we can only recall 25 percent of what was said. Solution: take quick notes on key points for later.

Ten: Acknowledge and praise creative ideas you get from listening. One way to build a culture of innovation is to create a recognition award devoted exclusively to celebrating creative suggestions. Give 'Great Idea' awards during monthly or quarterly get-togethers and they will powerfully underline the fact that supervisors are listening carefully to workers. A quick write-up in your company's newsletter is another great way to recognize innovative employee contributions.

CHAPTER FIVE

The Magical Power of Empathy and How To Use It

The Bottom Line: In the last chapter, we saw how listening effectively is the first step on the road to building a *WOW!* **Workplace** that can increase loyalty and boost productivity for any organization. But the next step – learning how to respond to employees with the kind of emotional intelligence that psychologists call empathy – is just as important. Here's why.

Got a tissue handy? Good, because you're probably going to need it as you read the following true story of how empathy in the workplace changed lives, shaped an employee's loyalty, and deeply impacted an entire organization.

Chrysler Makes a Friend for Life

It began in a Detroit suburb around eight o'clock on a muggy July evening when an 11-year-old girl named Sarah McPharlin dove underwater at her neighborhood swimming pool.

Although Sarah and her family could never have imagined it at the time, they were about to begin a journey that would become a legend in the annals of employee recognition.

"Mom, I've got a bad headache," Sarah had told her mother moments before taking the plunge on that warm summer night. "I'm gonna stick my head under and cool it off."

Dianne McPharlin nodded. "OK, honey. I hope that helps."

A moment later, the child was dipping beneath the surface of the community swimming pool.

But then she suddenly went limp and a stream of bright silver bubbles began to flow from her nose and mouth. Puzzled, the child's mother watched her drift aimlessly through the water.

Ten seconds passed. She's clowning around, Dianne thought with a flash of irritation. Hurriedly, she reached for her daughter's arm and pulled the limp sixth-grader to the surface.

"Sarah, cut it out. You're scaring me!"

No response.

"Sarah, I'm not kidding around. . . ."

Then, Dianne saw the water gushing from her child's nose. Alarmed, she pulled her daughter closer and shook her.

Nothing.

Sarah was unconscious. Her throat and lungs were full of water; in fact, she was in the early stages of drowning.

My God, thought Dianne McPharlin, a special education teacher. Oh, my God.

She began to shout for help. Within a matter of seconds, two lifeguards had pulled Sarah from her mother's anguished grasp and were administering CPR.

Numb with horror, Dianne stood helpless above the scene. Was this really happening to her child? Stunned and stricken, she listened to the wailing singsong of the approaching sirens. Hurry, she prayed as the lifeguards worked frantically to revive the ashen-faced child on the deck. For God's sake, please hurry!

An Employer with a Heart

While Dianne rode in the ambulance with her unconscious child, Sarah's older sister was frantically telephoning her father.

Jim McPharlin, a business analyst in the Product Development Department at Chrysler Motors in Detroit, listened to his older daughter with shock and then raced to the hospital.

There he learned that his ailing child was struggling with an ECHO virus that had attacked the electrical circuits in her heart and she had developed giant cell myocarditis. Her heart had been badly damaged. For the next three months, the suffering child would hover between life and death; her doctors concluded that her only remaining hope was a heart transplant.

But finding the right heart somewhere in America – and then getting it safely back to Michigan while still viable – would be an enormous challenge.

Jim McPharlin was on the edge of despair, and decided to share his plight with his manager, Chrysler Executive Vice President - Procurement and Supply, Gary Valade.

Valade listened carefully to Jim's story. And he listened empathetically, which means he listened with a kind of emotional intelligence that goes far beyond mere logic and pity.

According to the latest psychological research, emotional intelligence involves both feeling and rational analysis, and it's much more powerful than either one alone. Why? By tuning in to what they hear while listening carefully to employees on both the emotional and the analytical level, effective business people are able to come up with uniquely imaginative solutions to problems that would not otherwise occur to them, according to the research.

And that's exactly what happened in the McPharlin case.

After listening carefully to McPharlin, Valade asked a question that would change his employee's life. "Jim, if you can find the heart you need for Sarah in time, would it help to use Chrysler's corporate jet to rush it back to the hospital for the transplant surgery?"

As he expressed his thanks, McPharlin's eyes were suddenly glittering with tears. Years later, Valade would try to capture the moment in a simple sentence, "We value our employees at Chrysler – and we want them to know that."

About two months after this conversation, the McPharlins' telephone rang.

It was the heart surgeon. "We think we have a heart for Sarah in New Orleans." McPharlin took a huge breath and raced to the hospital. The hospital immediately dialed the number for the transportation unit at Chrysler.

And so the race began. Within 80 minutes, the Chrysler pilot was thundering down a runway accompanied by a pediatric cardiologist from the hospital.

They had about five hours in which to accomplish the transplant before the donated heart would begin to die. Once on the ground, the cardiologist determined that the donated heart was viable and the surgeons in Detroit began prepping Sarah for the potentially life-saving transplant.

It was a long and difficult surgery, but Sarah survived.

And since then, she has positively thrived.

As a high school senior, she would later become an enthusiastic runner on the school's cross-country team, and even go to the state finals in tennis. She would go on to win acceptance to Michigan State University.

And Dad? "Every day of my life," Jim McPharlin says, "I thank the folks at Chrysler for understanding what we were up against. I'm not exaggerating when I tell you that I've got a special place in my heart for this company, and that I come to work here every single day determined to give something back to an organization I love so much."

And what about Valade?

"We've got an outstanding HR department at Chrysler," he'll tell you with a quiet smile, "and I think that's because we do everything we can to recognize and appreciate our employees. We also try to listen to them with empathy because we know that if we show them we really care, the result will be a dedicated, inspired workforce that will want to stay with us for a lifetime."

Empathy: How It Can Enhance Recognition

It's a scientific fact, says one of America's best-known psychological researchers: the ability to use emotional intelligence – or empathy – is more helpful in developing effective employee management skills than mere analytical intelligence or a high I.Q.

"A lot of managers are surprised to discover this, but the data shows that emotional intelligence is actually far more important than cognitive [logical] intelligence when it comes to managing employees effectively," says bestselling psychologist Daniel Goleman, Ph.D., the author of *Emotional Intelligence: Why It Can Matter More Than IQ*.

Adds Dr. Goleman, who reviewed more than 500 workplace surveys from organizations scattered all around the globe while doing research for his groundbreaking book, "When it comes to measuring the qualities needed to motivate employees, the numbers are clear, and they tell us that possessing emotional intelligence matters at least twice as much as possessing technical or analytical skill. And the higher people move up in an organization, the more important this emotional intelligence becomes.

"The important thing to remember here is that while your IQ

remains relatively stable throughout life, the emotional skills required for effective management of employees can be learned. For that reason, it's crucial for business people and organizational managers to work on getting better at this."

While describing how such emotional intelligence can powerfully impact employees (with quantifiable gains in loyalty and productivity as the result), Dr. Goleman notes that empathy is actually a form of recognition that speaks to the whole person rather than merely to the employee of an organization. Goleman also says that more and more business leaders are catching on to this distinction, creating an interesting new HR trend: the increasing willingness of organizational managers to be proactive in helping valued employees deal with the personal challenges they face. Some remarkable examples:

In Scottsdale, Arizona, managers at Creative Healthcare Solutions, a small biotech and pharmaceutical marketing firm, responded to the sudden military call-up of their valued employee, Thomas P. Weikert, by making up the difference in his salary and continuing his employee benefits, including a retirement plan and healthcare for his family. In addition they provided the U.S. Army Reserve Lieutenant Colonel with monthly care packages that were shipped to his unit on duty in Iraq.

Weikert's empathetic bosses even flew to Atlanta to treat his two young sons to a Thrashers hockey game, complete with personalized jerseys, autographed pucks, and their names on the scoreboard. "They really went above and beyond," says an amazed Lt. Col. Weikert, "in terms of supporting not only me but also my family. As an employee, that's the kind of thing you don't forget."

For their actions on behalf of LTC Weikert and his family, the

Secretary of Defense presented CHS with the ESGR Employer Support Freedom Award.

In Miami, Florida, a highly skilled employee, whose home was about to be repossessed as part of the sub-prime mortgage mess, got the shock of her life. Her employer, a five-hospital, not-for-profit healthcare organization (Baptist Health South Florida), stepped in to offer her an unexpected $5,000 loan. Said the immensely relieved worker, a single mom who managed to stave off the foreclosure with the loan, "If it wasn't for Baptist, I don't know where I'd be right now." At the hospital group, meanwhile, officials pointed out that the empathetic response to their employee's plight made perfectly good business sense because she was a valued worker whose unique skills were greatly appreciated.

In Woodcliff Lake, New Jersey: Remember Wendy Jacob from Chapter 1? A veteran HR leader at BMW headquarters in the U.S., she astonished a troubled employee by intervening in a difficult parenting problem. As it turned out, the employee's second-grade son was struggling with behavior issues at his grade school, and the child's continuing inability to concentrate on schoolwork was interfering with his mom's on-the-job performance. During more than 30 years as an HR professional, Jacob has learned how to listen. After hearing the worried mother out, she suspected vision problems, and put the distracted employee in touch with an eye doctor who specialized in eye muscle therapy that helps kids with focusing problems to zero in on the classroom blackboard. Problem solved. When the boy's behavior and school performance improved, his grateful mom thanked Jacob profusely, and was able to be re-energized for her work responsibilities.

"Empathy is important," says the BMW manager, "but it has to be about finding solutions and not just about expressing sympathy. I really think the key to developing emotional intelligence is to work hard at combining your ability to feel for employees with lots of self-education about resources and tools. So when the time comes, the solutions to their problems will be there for you."

Building Empathy: Five Winning Strategies

Did you know that the word empathy comes to us from the ancient Greek term *empatheia*, which simply means passion?

And did you also know that the ability to imagine the reality of others – to empathize – is a key ingredient in building the kind of recognition culture that can improve worker productivity and motivation in any organization?

It's true, and here are five simple methods any business person can use to get better at empathizing.

One: Ask yourself, "What if?" During discussions with an employee, try to imagine what it would be like to change places with this person. What would happen if you had to deal with these issues, and how would you feel about them? What would you want to hear? By using this kind of imaginative projection, you can become much better as a listener while helping workers to find problem solutions for themselves.

Two: Learn how to slow yourself down during conversations. Given the fierce time pressures of the contemporary workplace, it's easy to fall into the habit of glossing over an employee who's going through a difficult time. But hurrying through a conversation with an agitated employee won't allow much time for empathy. Instead, realize that part of being an effective manager is noticing and responding to your people on a personal level. When you learn about an employee going through a rough patch at work or in his or her personal life, discipline yourself to slow down so your emotional responses to what you're hearing can emerge spontaneously.

Three: Don't try to be "Mr. (or Ms.) Fixit." Instead of trying to find instant, magical solutions for employee problems, admit openly that you're not a magician while pointing out that you are sincerely interested in learning more about the person in front of you. Share that you'd like to help – if possible. Quite often, you'll discover that what the employee needs most of all is the empathy rather than a quick fix for the problem.

Four: Don't unload your own baggage. Although it's tempting to start yammering about your own problems with a troubled employee, switching the spotlight to yourself will only dilute your role as an empathetic listener. For best results, limit your responses to comments about the employee's issues and not your own.

Five: Never make snap judgments. Responding to others with empathy means listening to them with heightened emotion and awareness, not becoming a cheerleader for their biases and emotionally charged opinions. Your strategy should be to ask questions whenever possible, rather than making pronouncements. For example, you might ask an angry employee: "Why do you think your boss' recent comment is bothering you so much?" (Instead of blurting out something like, "Why, your boss had absolutely no right to say that to you.") In most cases, you'll find that if you stick with questions, you won't be drawn into making inappropriate comments about the situation at hand.

CHAPTER SIX

Putting Together a Winning Recognition Strategy: The Basics

The Bottom Line: Now that we have a clear fix on the exciting opportunities that can be generated by establishing a ***WOW!* Workplace** using recognition within your organization, it's time to roll up our sleeves and start building a program that can earn maximum results. The process may look complicated at first, but it actually requires only a few simple steps as you'll see in this chapter.

Some Amazing Results at Stanley Tools

Brian Hicks feels very strongly about how important it is to let his employees know how much he values them. "Absolutely, it's important," booms the South Region Manager for Stanley Proto Industrial Tools, one of this country's most recognized hand-tool brands. Then he adds: "Positively. Without a doubt."

Obviously, Hicks is a huge fan of well-run employee recognition programs – and for good reason. Since 2003, he says, his total sales volume has been growing at nearly 25 percent per year, in large part because of the incredible energy generated by a company sales team that seems to "grow more loyal and dedicated to our mission" with each passing day.

According to Hicks, the continuing sales growth at the Tennessee-based Stanley Proto Industrial Tools South Region isn't happening by accident. He says, "I think we're very fortunate in this office because we learned a long time ago that people are the greatest asset any company has to offer.

"We really value our sales and support staff, and we let them know it by recognizing their major accomplishments and their special service milestones in a way that really makes an impression. But we also let them know how much we appreciate their efforts in an informal way, and that kind of informal recognition process goes on around here constantly. As a result, our sales people are famous for rising to the occasion and meeting almost any challenge we throw at them."

To illustrate his point, Hicks leans back in his office chair and launches into one of his favorite activities – telling a good story.

"A couple of years ago," Hicks begins, "we landed a very large account here in Tennessee. That was great news and we were thrilled. But I also realized that we were going to be challenged to provide this client with the very best service we could deliver."

"Realizing that, I started thinking about all the guys on our team. Then I selected the one I thought was most capable of meeting the challenge. I called him into my office and I told him, 'Jerry, if there's anybody on this sales force who can handle this tough account flawlessly, it's you.'

"And he did. Because I had recognized his abilities like that – expressing complete confidence in him – Jerry took the assignment to heart. He worked very hard to prove me right. As a result, this account continues to bring us new business every month, and it all happened because of the recognition he received."

First Step: Define Your Organization's Mission

Ever heard that wonderful, old Chinese proverb? *The longest journey begins with a single step.*

When it comes to building a successful recognition strategy, the crucially important first step is to sit down and review your mission statement in order to gain a sharp focus on your organization's goals and aspirations. This allows you to build your recognition program around these key objectives.

"You'd be surprised how many HR managers and other organizational administrators haven't really taken the time to think about their mission statement," says longtime management consultant Pat Dillon, who's based near Portland, Oregon. "But if you think about it, getting on top of the mission statement is really essential because everything starts there."

To understand how important it is to link your company's overall mission with its recognition strategy, just look at the official mission statement for McDonald's, which operates more than 30,000 thriving fast-food restaurants around the world:

The McDonald's vision is to be the world's best quick service restaurant experience. Being the best means providing outstanding quality, service, cleanliness and value, so that we make every customer in every restaurant smile.

At McDonald's, long regarded as one of the smartest retail food marketers in the world, that mission statement dovetails perfectly with an employee awards program that rewards workers for living up to every word in the statement every single day. As numerous observers have pointed out through the years, Mickey D has carefully thought through both its mission and the awards it uses to promote the accomplishment of that mission.

Understanding the Three Legs of Recognition

Having reviewed and clarified your organizational goals by thinking about your mission statement, the next step in building a powerhouse recognition strategy is to begin thinking about the three basic forms of employee recognition: formal, informal, and day-to-day.

Like the three legs on a perfectly balanced stool, these three different kinds of recognition will serve as the rock-solid foundation on which you can build or expand your organization's recognition strategy. We'll start with an introduction to each, and in the next few chapters, we'll explore the ins and outs of all three forms in detail.

Formal Recognition: These programs frequently involve length-of-service or structured performance awards that are presented to deserving employees in order to acknowledge and honor significant career achievements. The formal leg in the recognition stool is critical to the stability of your recognition initiative for two very important reasons:

1) It objectively ensures that recognition is tied to the goals that you have outlined, and

2) It provides the solid structure that will ensure your program is consistent day after day, year after year.

That consistency is absolutely essential when it comes to building an effective recognition strategy because formal recognition gives both managers and employees a framework so that everyone is on the same page. Everyone understands what employees need to do to be recognized.

When a formal recognition program is working right, there's a sense of anticipation as employees work toward the milestones and achievement goals that have been established, and there is a true celebration when those goals are reached.

I was in New England recently to give a seminar on employee recognition to a group of business folks there. Afterward, a woman in the audience came up to me and said, "We started a recognition program two years ago. We gave our managers a budget to recognize their teams. It went great for a couple of months, but then fizzled out, and now our employees are discouraged. How can I keep my company's managers committed to giving recognition consistently?"

I've been asked this question dozens of times in the last couple of years. The fact is, even with the best of intentions, managers who are struggling to "get everything done" can be distracted and forget about this aspect of good employee relations. The result, all too often, is that recognition gets put on the back burner, which frequently backfires by compromising the energy and creativity of even the best teams.

It is precisely at this point that an effectively run formal recognition program can save the day by taking the guesswork out of the process and by helping managers to maintain a program that has built-in continuity. This ensures that presentations of length-of-service and performance awards in addition to other kinds of formal recognition will occur on a regular timetable. Most important, it ensures that employees who have worked hard to achieve recognition will not be overlooked. In this way, the thorny problem of forgetting about recognition until it's too late is nicely solved – bringing peace of mind and certainty to the process. Thanks to this assured consistency, both managers and employees can be certain of reaping the many benefits that result from effective recognition.

Formal recognition presentations can be designed to serve as occasions for:

- *Honoring years of service milestones*
- *Presenting sales incentives*
- *Rewarding achievements*
- *Establishing and rewarding quality standards*
- *Acknowledging successful completion of projects*
- *Recognizing successful completion of training programs*
- *Honoring outstanding customer service*
- *Recognizing steady attendance*

Informal Recognition: Although this type of employee recognition doesn't always require significant investments, informal acknowledgement of employees is extremely important in building a culture of recognition. (See Chapter Eight.) Whether you send handwritten congratulatory notes to an employee who's making noticeable contributions or invite a special projects team over to your backyard for a barbecue, it isn't as important as using this method of recognition frequently, consistently, and with plenty of public acknowledgment for the employees you're applauding with your informal nod of approval.

Over the years, I've become a huge fan of this creative method for showing your co-workers just how much you value and appreciate them. And I never stop being amazed at how powerful this tool can be.

Only the other day, for example, I heard about a company in the Midwest that recognized a team of employees who had been working on a grueling, time-consuming assignment. The group's supervisor expressed appreciation for the long hours of dedication to the project by arranging a trip to the local minor league ballpark for batting practice. When the workers arrived on the field, the supervisor presented each one with a personalized jersey and a heartfelt thanks.

As you might expect, the batting practice was a hit with the entire group and a perfect way to blow off steam. This creative gesture of appreciation bolstered the weary employees' spirits, and they returned to work ready to tackle the project with fresh energy and hit it out of the park. There are a thousand different strategies like this that HR leaders can employ to make informal recognition a successful element in their overall strategy.

Informal recognition can be a tremendously effective way to provide your employees with ongoing encouragement as they progress toward the significant milestones and achievements which are commemorated by your formal recognition initiatives. Among the opportunities for informal recognition, a handful of ideas include:

- *On-the-spot recognition for extra effort and contributions*
- *Peer-to-peer recognition*
- *Points-based recognition*
- *Celebrations for project milestones*
- *Commemoration of personal holidays*

Day-To-Day Recognition: It can be as simple as a quick telephone call or a spontaneous visit to an employee's work-littered desk or manufacturing bench. Or it may mean taking the time and trouble to learn every employee's name and the key details that matter most in that person's life.

As I can tell you from personal experience, there's something magical about what happens when you ask a valued employee how he fared in that regional amateur tennis tournament or how his son is doing on the local high school football team.

But there's no magic involved in mastering this form of recognition. To get it right, a business person or HR manager has to be energetic and honestly curious about the lives of the people who work at his or her organization. One of the things I often tell HR folks is that you can't fake recognition – ever.

People are very astute when it comes to personal interactions. After nearly two decades of managing people in a variety of settings, I can assure you that employees can see right through pretense – the first time and every time.

That means that in order to build a culture that truly believes in genuine and ongoing recognition of employees, you have to care about your workers as human beings. You have to invest the time and energy required to get to know them on more than the surface level. And most of all, you have to respect what I call the "deep depth" of their rich, multi-dimensional lives.

Get those things right, and you'll be able to build a ***WOW!*** **Workplace** with enough power to light up Texas Stadium for a night game.

And in the next three chapters, we're going to show you exactly how to do that.

Using Recognition To Improve Performance: Nine Strategies

It's a fact: human beings perform better when other people praise them, express confidence in them, reward them appropriately, and then challenge them to go beyond their current level of performance.

As the managing partner of one of the world's most experienced employee recognition consulting firms, I've had the honor of watching the same extraordinary phenomenon unfold over and over again.

The scenario: A manager is faced with a situation in which an employee is underperforming in some aspect of his or her job. But instead of merely scolding the worker, the astute manager finds a way to recognize some positive aspect of the employee's performance and then challenges that individual to do a better job at the task under review.

If you want to see just how powerful this approach to enhancing job performance can be, try following this checklist of time-tested recognition strategies.

ONE: Design a highly positive recognition moment – maybe a sit-down exchange over a cup of coffee – when you follow your praise with a specific, precisely detailed challenge. Example: "You did a terrific job of leading the quality control meeting last week, Bill, which tells me you're more than ready to meet the challenge of helping the team reach our goal of reducing defects by seven percent next month." With a face-to-face exchange, you can be sure that there will be no misunderstanding about the sincerity of your praise or about your expectations for improved performance. By leading off with a positive message of support, you create a safe haven within which the worker can feel confident about the chances for future success on the job.

TWO: Always send a message of confidence and not doubt. "We know you can do it, Bill, which is precisely why we tapped you for this project."

THREE: Include an opportunity for helpful training or education as part of the recognition process. Make the training a reward rather than a punishment. Try, "We're excited about what you accomplished last month, and this additional training will help you take it to the next level and grow your career."

FOUR: Go public with your recognition and your challenge for the under-performing employee. At meetings and planning sessions, go out of your way to express confidence in the struggling individual. Make sure the worker's peers see how you're praising his or her more positive efforts even as you call for further improvement in other areas. Be honest and praise only those efforts that truly deserve recognition.

A terrific example of how going public can hold individuals accountable to performance goals comes from my good friend Sarah Reinertsen, a fellow triathlon fanatic. Sarah spoke about motivation and achieving goals at one of our recent Terryberry North American sales meetings. The gritty

Reinertsen – the first woman amputee ever to complete the Ironman Triathlon – told her amazed listeners how she gains extra drive and motivation by informing friends and family about her latest physical goals. "Once I go public with my goals," she said, "I realize that I had better dig down and find the strength and endurance I need to actually achieve them." In the same way, public encouragement can energize an employee to work to meet expectations.

FIVE: Make sure the challenge you present is realistic, measurable and achievable. Don't send a handwritten note saying: "We need to get orders out much faster from your manufacturing group." Instead, say, "I'm betting you can speed up production lead time by 10 percent – or even more – if you spend some time reviewing your schedules and procedures."

SIX: Always follow up your recognition-linked challenges with careful measurement and prompt acknowledgement of gains. Try, "I know you've been working hard at making improvements in this area, and your report last week showed that. Can we do a quick review of your overall progress next Monday?"

SEVEN: Create a public kudos page in your organization's newsletter, Intranet posting or bulletin board display space. Then use this feature to praise improvements in targeted problems, emphasizing the progress. As the employee you're trying to help begins to meet your challenges, fire off occasional one-liners for the kudos page, such as, "We hear that Bill Smith is well along in his continuing campaign to speed up our accounting processes for invoicing. Now, we're wondering if he and his team can top their recent gains and do even better next month? Stay tuned."

Of course, you can also offer peers the opportunity to post ideas and kudos. Remember, the praise doesn't have to come from management only. Truly effective recognition comes from all levels of an organization – and it's contagious.

EIGHT: Don't forget about employees who are performing. As in most management situations, balance is everything and that means keeping a vigilant eye out for opportunities to praise high-performers along with trying to motivate those who lag behind. Praise for high-performers puts the spotlight on the level of expectation you have for all employees. Essentially, the praise says, "This is what we're after," setting the performance standard for the entire organization.

NINE: Motivate by rewarding incrementally as the employee reaches progress points in a carefully designed set of realistic, step-by-step accomplishments. How? Simply break down your overall improvement goal into stages and then award the employee with points or "XYZ Bucks" for reaching each stage along his or her journey toward the ultimate goal. Allow the employee to accumulate and redeem the points for special awards. This framework provides positive and encouraging moments during the course of an extended project while motivating the individual to continue to work toward larger and more productive goals.

CHAPTER SEVEN

Building A Winning Formal Recognition Strategy

The Bottom Line: Now that we've established a firm grip on the organizational mission statement, it's time to take the next step on the road to the *WOW!* **Workplace** by establishing a powerful formal recognition program. Most top employers start with a foundation based on honoring their people's years of service, but they don't stop there. It's important to expand your recognition efforts to honor performance achievements. You'll find that you need to start by mastering a few basics. Here they are:

A Limo Ride for the McDonald's Manager

From the moment the jet-black limousine greeted her at the airport until the end of the evening, Melissa Snider couldn't stop saying, "Wow!" This hard-working McDonald's restaurant manager was a tireless leader with a knack for building loyalty and dedication among her devoted crew members. But tonight was her night. The limo ride was only the beginning of an unforgettable evening. It was an evening devoted to her and to recognizing Snider's contribution to McDonald's.

Imagine her excitement when the big luxury car pulled up in front of a downtown hotel where she was the guest of honor at a special awards banquet to recognize her exceptional management skills.

During the ceremonies that ensued, the gifted McDonald's manager would receive a sterling-silver, inscribed plaque, a special, gold McDonald's lapel pin and several other uniquely valuable gifts.

As the winner of a highly esteemed Ray Kroc Excellence Award, Snider was about to earn the ultimate in formal recognition – these coveted trophy-like items that beautifully symbolize the respect and affection her bosses felt for her as one of their most effective managers.

And her reaction?

"I felt like I was on a red carpet," Snider told a reporter during the awards ceremony. "I rode to the presentation in a limousine provided by McDonald's, and when I got there, I found half a dozen regional managers waiting to salute me."

Then, with a glowing smile that spoke volumes about the power of formal recognition to help create a *WOW!* **Workplace**, Snider summed up her experience as a valued and appreciated employee, "That awards ceremony felt like attending the Oscars."

Formal Recognition: The ABCs

As one who's been fortunate to spend a lot of time talking with highly accomplished business leaders and HR administrators, I've come to appreciate the enormous psychological power that can be generated by formal recognition. In situation after situation, I've seen that power light up the eyes – and the brilliant smiles – of workers who positively glowed with good energy, after receiving a recognition award that beautifully symbolized the esteem their colleagues felt for them.

While observing these highly emotional and rewarding moments, I've often asked myself why they seem to hold such extraordinary emotional power for almost everyone involved. I've also interviewed a wide variety of psychologists, sociologists and motivational consultants in an effort to account for the huge amounts of emotional energy that are released during these ceremonial recognition occasions.

One key insight that emerged quickly from my research has to do with the symbolic aspect of the physical award presented to honorees. For reasons that lie buried deep in the psychology of our species, human beings have a remarkable ability to focus their feelings on objects. (If you don't believe me, just walk into any jewelry store during May or June and check out all the shoppers pricing engagement or wedding rings!)

I'm certainly not a trained psychologist . . . but it does seem pretty clear to me that people usually value the symbol much more than the object itself. How many times have you heard professional football players vow during interviews that they will "do whatever it takes" to win a Super Bowl ring, and that they won't think about retiring until they've finally won the diamond-studded, solid-gold status symbol?

Most of these super-athletes earn several million dollars a year and could buy any number of diamond-studded rings without worrying about the cost.

But that wouldn't be the point. These super jocks don't care about the object; they want what it symbolizes, which is nothing less than the ultimate achievement in their field, along with the respect, esteem and admiration of the professional football world.

Describing this esteem factor as the foundation for any

recognition program that hopes to have a significant impact on workers, one of North America's most frequently quoted workplace psychologists points to research showing that if they are to be effective, recognition awards must symbolically embody the esteem they are meant to convey.

"There's no doubt that the real power of the engraved crystal or the custom watch a worker receives as a recognition award lies in its ability to convey esteem," says Donald R. Soeken, Ph.D., a Washington, D.C.-area psychologist who often advises workplace managers on employee attitudes and employee recognition. "And I think its most lasting value can be found in the way it will go on reminding the recipient of a moment when supervisors and co-workers paused to acknowledge the esteem they felt for that individual."

Along with the respect factor, the other all-important aspect of a good award lies in its ability to become the icon of the achievement which an individual has worked so hard to attain. Like Dr. Soeken, I'm convinced that understanding the inner dynamics of employee recognition is the most effective way to build a culture in which all of the members of an organization are valued and respected for their contributions.

Introducing the "Big 3" of Formal Recognition

Here, then, is the central concept on which the success of any formal recognition program will ultimately depend:

In order to achieve maximum impact with any recognition award, you must make sure that it powerfully expresses the symbolic meaning it is meant to convey.

To accomplish that supremely important objective, you have to make a few basic choices that will determine both your selection of the physical awards and your method of presentation. To simplify the process, let's break the planning process down into the "Big 3" elements of recognition awards.

ONE: The perceived value: You must make sure that the award's symbolic value to the recipient is as high as possible. In other words, you need to think carefully – perhaps with the help of a recognition advisor or consultant, if possible – about what the chosen item represents. Consider what message you want to send by giving that personalized writing instrument, top-end fly fishing set, or charm bracelet with your company symbol. Would you give an inscribed coffee mug as an award meant to honor 10 years of service with the same organization? Definitely not. A contribution of that scope demands a unique award that conveys a profound feeling of respect and appreciation – not a token coffee mug.

TWO: The business value: It's essential, of course, that your award supports the goals of your business by making a connection between your honoree's contribution and your group's mission. Getting this right demands that you think your way through the awards process carefully in order to make sure every award you give (whether for years of service, sales contribution, or some other performance measure) works to advance your organizational goals to the maximum. For example, though most employees like that green paper, cash is actually unsuitable as a recognition award. Why? For one very simple reason: there is nothing intrinsic about cash that builds that valuable connection between your business and your employee. Money is evaporative. It gets spent and then forgotten, leaving nothing behind to remind the employee why he or she was singled out for special recognition.

THREE: The presentation of the award to the recipient: When putting together a formal recognition program (and I can't underline this enough), it's extremely important to understand that the way the award is presented will affect the ultimate impact as much as the physical award itself. According to the latest research in organizational development, the experience of the presentation – and the extent to which the remarks are successful at connecting the individual, his or her achievement, and the business' goals - will directly shape the worker's perception of the award and, ultimately, the effectiveness of your recognition efforts.

So there you have them: The Big 3 of formal recognition. Take the time and trouble to plan your awards around perceived value, make sure they dovetail perfectly with your organizational mission, and then, finally, put together some knockout presentations that will drive your message home with clarity and emotion. You are now well on your way to building the kind of *WOW!* **Workplace** that can transform your organization and motivate everyone in your shared enterprise.

Now you have the lowdown on the formal side of recognition. But what's the best way to start working on the informal side, putting together a high-performing program for recognizing the contributions of employees in a continuing way in order to maintain that culture in between your formal events? In Chapter Eight, we'll explore some clever strategies (and meet some very clever business leaders) who've been able to do just that by thinking long and hard about the process of informal recognition.

Formal Recognition Events: Dos And Don'ts

What's the best way to make sure that the formal recognition event you're planning achieves maximum impact?

"When an awards banquet, luncheon or other event goes well, everyone involved benefits," says Greg Butterfield, an Atlanta-based recognition and engagement professional with 27 years of experience. "If the presentation is heartfelt and genuine, everybody in the room will come away feeling positive and uplifted."

But the flip side of that statement is also true; if your awards event falls flat, it could end up de-motivating the very people it was meant to inspire.

To make sure that doesn't happen to your formal recognition event, observe these 12 dos and don'ts.

DO make sure to put the presentation of any award before all else as you plan a banquet, luncheon or other formal recognition event. Sure, it's important to create a pleasing backdrop with a good choice of venue and good food, etc., but research shows that what people usually remember most is the way the awards were presented to them and what was said about their efforts and achievements. The physical award serves to remind the recipient later of both the presentation experience and the achievement. If resources are limited, it's more important to put your energy into the presentation than into the physical details of the gathering.

DON'T be content with limiting your guest list to the award recipients' co-workers. Why? The guest list is crucially important and requires careful planning. When possible, make sure recipients' families and close friends are invited in addition to as many higher-ups as possible from your organization.

DO choose the right presenter. Their words are a powerful opportunity to make a lasting impact – whether positive or negative – on a valuable employee. That's why it's essential to choose a presenter who is knowledgeable about what the individual has accomplished and how it impacts your business. A Terryberry best practice: choose the highest-ranking individual in your organization who has a personal connection to the recipient. An employee's immediate supervisor is almost always a good choice as this person knows the individual, the job, and what constitutes "above and beyond." For especially noteworthy achievements, perhaps you'd like to invite a couple of individuals who interact with the recipient to say a few words.

DON'T be vague. The more specific you can be in your comments about the recipient's special qualities, skills and accomplishments, the more impact your message will have. Share details about ways that the individual has contributed to the mission, goals and objectives of your business. This is essential; it reinforces, to both the honoree and others in attendance, what attributes and behaviors the organization values. The presenter should also be careful to explain the basis of the award so that everyone in attendance will see the link between the achievement involved and the symbol that honors it. By verbally reinforcing the special qualities and the symbolic significance of the award, presenters will help to establish the award's residual effect, giving you much more bang for the buck long after the event is over.

DO make absolutely certain that the presenter of the awards is prepared with a clear, accurate outline of all the specifics and has reviewed the information prior to the event. You want to make certain that names will be pronounced correctly and all work-history details and other biographical info will be 100 percent accurate.

DON'T neglect the message you are sending to the rest of the employees in attendance. As you plan and conduct your event, it's helpful to remember that while the occasion is designed to honor and salute a deserving employee, everyone else will also take away a valuable experience. Ever seen a group of sportsfans brought together by their favorite team's big win? Ever been moved and motivated by watching an Olympic athlete receive a gold medal? The same applies to your workplace. Create a moment of honor for a deserving employee, and it can serve as a powerful motivating experience for all. You should leave no doubt in attendees' minds about what they will need to do if they are to earn recognition the next time around.

DO keep the focus on the award recipients. Make sure the presenters don't try to use the event to make windy speeches about the wonders of the organization involved, but rather how the recipient's efforts support the company mission. This may require some diplomacy on your part. One way to make the point is to simply remind presenters, "We're on a very tight schedule, so please keep your remarks limited to the award recipients."

DON'T arrange for a recognition award to be delivered to a recipient's home or workplace without presentation if you can avoid it. Since the physical presentation of the award establishes the connection between the award and the achievement, it's best to make sure all awards are presented in person. An award casually left on an employee's chair or tossed in the mailbox will lose some of its lustre. If the selected award is too large to present in person, or if the award is intangible, consider using a small symbolic item that will serve as a stand-in and show that you put some thought into it. One of the fastest growing award trends today is the use of presentation kits. Often packaged in an attractive box, these kits contain a certificate or plaque and a small memento to provide the recipient with something tangible to connect with the recognition experience.

DO help your award recipients plan and prepare for the event. Tell them what to expect, and make suggestions about what to wear and whom to invite. Give them a schedule of the presentation event in advance, and then reassure them that there's nothing to be nervous about and it's going to be lots of fun. Recognize that not everyone enjoys the spotlight; make sure your remarks and presentation are in tune with the person being recognized.

DON'T wait too long after the achievement to arrange for public recognition. A timely presentation will have much more impact than one staged long after the high from the achievement has passed.

DO spend as much time as you can thinking about how you can best evoke the *WOW!* response during the presentation. How about displaying a jumbo-sized photo of the recipient that coworkers have inscribed with messages of appreciation? What about surprising the recipient by inviting a special associate from years past to say a few words about the honoree? We worked with one organization that had armed guards deliver a very special award to the podium to be presented. The sky's the limit – once you commit to going for that *WOW!* response.

DON'T forget to go after the maximum mileage from your formal recognition event by referring to it later – whenever possible. Send recipients a handwritten, day-after note: "That was a wonderful presentation last night; it was great to see you get the recognition you deserve." Or write an enthusiastic description of the event for your organization's newsletter or online publication. Remember that taking photos of the event and distributing them later can provide a powerful reminder for everyone involved.

CHAPTER EIGHT

Using Informal Recognition To Create a *WOW!* Workplace

The Bottom Line: Once you understand the enormous power of informal recognition, you can use it to create a work environment in which your newly energized people are free to be creative – and to challenge themselves (as well as each other) to reach new heights of productivity and service. Here's the lowdown on how to let this high-voltage form of recognition work for you.

A Mob Scene at the In-N-Out

As soon as the manager opened the door of the fast-food restaurant, a mob of eager high school and college students came rushing in.

But these bright-eyed and bushy-tailed young people – more than a hundred of them, as it turned out – weren't looking for cheeseburgers or French fries or strawberry milkshakes.

These guys wanted jobs.

As they swarmed into the fast-food eatery and began feverishly filling out applications, the manager and his astonished assistants shook their heads in wonder. Only a few days before, this same restaurant management crew had posted signs and run newspaper ads announcing that a total of 48 students would be hired in the next two days for part-time jobs.

And then came the shock.

During 48 hours of job interviews, more than 1,000 fired-up applicants materialized at the restaurant, and every single one of them expressed a burning desire to work as hamburger flippers or milkshake shakers, starting immediately.

An unlikely scenario? You bet. But it actually took place on a mild September morning a few years ago in the booming Los Angeles suburb of Alhambra, California (population: 85,000) after the remarkably successful fast-food chain known as In-N-Out Burger began hiring young people for a brand-new outlet.

And why did so many eager kids show up to apply?

According to numerous HR consultants and workplace analysts who later studied the employment stampede at the In-N-Out Burger, the overwhelming response was triggered by "enlightened personnel management policies" at the family-owned In-N-Out Burger, one of America's most successful restaurant enterprises.

As some of North America's most knowledgeable workplace observers have noted in recent years, the enterprising burger chain has been setting a new standard for progressive employment practices. The extraordinary saga of In-N-Out's takeoff during the past 10 years is a compelling reminder of the enormous business success that can be generated when an organization effectively addresses its workers' desire to feel a sense of gratification and belonging within the workplace community. And one key component of creating this exciting community environment is achieved by practicing effective informal employee recognition. Learn to be successful in this area and, like In-N-Out, you'll begin to create a workplace family in which associates are excited about their work community and their role within it.

Workplace experts such as Jack Deal, president of the highly regarded Deal Business Consulting group, have often been quoted on the subject of how In-N-Out staffers consider the daily informal recognition they receive to be "as important as compensation." But the most revealing insights have actually come from the young people who work for the fast-growing burger biz.

Take 21-year-old Bryan, for example, a college senior who blogged about his job. "As an employee, I LOVE working for In-N-Out. I've been there for three years and loving every day of it. They care for their employees SO much. We have events every year, which include a family picnic, bowling tournaments, softball tournaments, and golf tournaments. We also have a canned food drive during Christmas. I mean, the list goes on and on...I will continue to work at this place for a very long time."

Like hundreds of other workers at the surging enterprise, the youthful Bryan says he loves to come to work. How come? Because the enlightened people who manage the In-N-Out stores long ago figured out how to tap into the enormous power of informal recognition and then began using it to create a California-style version of the ultimate *WOW!* **Workplace.**

Of course, the formal recognition program at In-N-Out also ranks as one of the most innovative and creative of its kind today, says renowned management expert Patrick Lencioni. Not only do employees receive award plaques and small gifts (including colorful beach tote bags and cute In-N-Out stuffed animals after six months), but they also earn larger awards from a selection of items at one, three, and five years of service. In addition, both managers and hourly workers are eligible for customer-service awards that are presented once a year at many stores.

Combine these impressive formal awards with In-N-Out's ongoing program of informal recognition, and it's easy to see why hordes of young people show up regularly to work there.

To understand just how committed In-N-Out Burger is to recognizing and valuing all their employees, all you have to do is read the "History" entry on the fast-growing company's website.

In-N-Out remains privately owned and the Snyder family has no plans to take the company public or franchise any units. All Associates are treated like family. Many Associates have been with In-N-Out for over 20 years, some even worked with Harry and Esther (original founders of In-N-Out Burger) in the early years. These relationships and the commitment to the company's philosophies continue to make In-N-Out a very special place to work.

Flexible Recognition That Fuels Your Workers

So what's the best way to begin building your own uniquely original version of the smashingly successful In-N-Out informal recognition program?

The first step is to understand how informal and day-to-day recognition supports your formal recognition efforts to build a complete recognition culture. Remember the three-legged stool concept from Chapter Six? As we talked about a few pages ago, formal recognition commemorates significant contributions and milestones that stand out in an employee's career. Formal recognition programs are designed to honor those special achievements in a structured and consistent way. Informal recognition, on the other hand, is a more flexible and spontaneous form of recognition that celebrates special effort or above-and-beyond performance on a more frequent basis. If you'll indulge me for another Ironman Triathlon analogy, I think of informal recognition as the burrito I give myself as a reward after finishing a long training session while formal recognition is actually crossing that race's finish line and receiving my finisher's medal.

When it comes to informal recognition, of course, the good news is that it's creatively wide open, which means you can essentially design any kind of program you want based on the personality of your own, unique workforce. Some helpful examples:

---In many smaller to mid-size organizations, creative managers are finding ways to informally recognize high-performing employees. At one Northeastern University Pharmaceutical Sciences Laboratory in Boston, Massachusetts, Director Dr. Barbara Waszczak routinely rewards lab workers who come up with solutions to problems by bragging about their accomplishments in two different university science newsletters. Says Waszczak, "I want my people to know that I'm very aware of their contributions – and that if they solve a problem in the lab or find a new way to do something, it's going to get noticed."

---At a growing number of workplaces, employers are encouraging workers to engage in lots of healthy exercise. It's not uncommon for businesses to provide on-site workout rooms and daily exercise periods in which their people are given 30 minutes or so to get in better shape. Increasingly, workers who meet wellness goals are celebrated with healthy gift awards, such as pool memberships, new bicycles or sporty clothing. In effect, employees are being recognized for contributing to their organization by remaining healthy.

---Another surging trend is hosting regular social events for teams of workers who are engaged in special projects that require them to work together for extended periods of time. Of course, the form of these team-building activities is as varied as human nature itself. In Kansas City, for example, a locally based travel agency takes groups of successful sales people to lunch on the company at a famed steak house once a month. An Atlanta printing firm hosts a whitewater rafting adventure where team members truly learn how to work together.

---At many smaller companies around the country, managers are joining a growing trend of hosting backyard cookouts or informal dinner parties for key employees. While the low cost of these social events is easily managed, the reservoir of goodwill they generate can be huge, and can literally last for years. Says a mid-size electronics company manager in Louisville, Kentucky, who frequently employs this informal recognition strategy, "When people socialize by sharing a meal on the weekend, they tend to bond in a way that energizes and enriches their teamwork."

---In a functional "workplace family," recognition doesn't just come from the top down. In the most successful workplaces, peers also acknowledge and support each other for performing well. At a manufacturing facility in Ohio, employees have created the "Big Fish" program. A huge laminated picture of a fish bowl takes up a bulletin board in their lunch area. When an employee wants to acknowledge the contribution of a coworker, he or she writes the honoree's name on a fish-shaped piece of paper and pins it inside the fishbowl. The Big Fish is then honored with lots of high fives and fist bumps from peers.

Like most other successful human endeavors, the art of informal recognition requires plenty of thoughtfulness, creativity, and plain old common sense. But it isn't complicated and most of us can get it right. All we need is a willingness to use our imaginations to design activities, events or presentations that will leave the members of our organizations uttering that wonderful word, *WOW!*

To accomplish that exciting goal, all that's really required is to be able to imagine the daily reality of your workers. Then, you will be able to invent and implement shared activities (a summertime badminton tournament to celebrate the successful launch of a project or a fishing outing for the team's children at a local lake?) that will recognize their great value and worth in a relaxed and authentic way.

For Informal Recognition: 10 Power Boosters

When it comes to the fine art of informal recognition, the key word to remember is: *Frequency.*

The impact of informal recognition arises from the consistent, positive reinforcement that occurs after you reach organizational objectives. Generally, these types of achievements don't require significant monetary investment. But they do take an investment of time since this form of recognition demands that you give frequent acknowledgement of contributions by workers. As is the case with formal recognition, putting the appropriate structure in place to ensure timely and consistent informal praise and recognition of your people will help to guarantee success.

Need a boost to get started informally? Here are 10 ideas businesses are using.

ONE: Create a compliment bulletin board where you and your employees can post positive comments about co-workers. This feature adds an element of old-fashioned fun to the office environment. It also puts your attaboys and attagirls on wide display while encouraging others to participate in the *WOW!* **Workplace** you're developing.

TWO: Develop a peer-to-peer recognition program that allows employees to have a hand in deciding who is honored with significant awards. Place a nomination box in your common area, and create a simple form that can be used to recommend colleagues who are contributing at a high level. More and more businesses are using online programs for this. Team members can make nominations right from their computers, and nominees are immediately notified that someone noticed their contribution. The key thing here is to make sure that both the people who are nominated and those who recommend them are informed of the award winners in a way that enthusiastically praises their contributions.

THREE: Cut the ties. An auto dealer in Toledo has long enjoyed a unique tradition that seems especially powerful as a recognition-enhancer. When a new salesperson sells his first car, all his colleagues gather around while the sales manager snips his tie with a pair of scissors. After the tie has been severed at the knot, it's pinned to the wall in the achiever's office in the midst of a triumphant ceremony. Tour the dealership and you'll find the "tie trophies" proudly displayed in the offices of veteran sales people, often many years after they were snipped. Unique informal ceremonies like this help to establish your culture and make it memorable.

FOUR: Invest in a box of Snickers® and some Avery® Labels. For instant availability, keep the box of candy bars in your office drawer (remember, they're not for afternoon snacks), and hand the goodies out along with your praise for a job well done. To achieve even more pizzazz, use your computer to print colorful labels with your company logo and mission. After attaching them to the Snickers® treats, hand out an "ABC Company Excellence Bar" each time you catch an employee doing something great to support your mission.

FIVE: Develop a motivating phrase that will instantly convey your mission statement during a particular timeframe (week, month, or season). Example: August is customer service excellence month! Now, make that great phrase part of a colorful poster and plant it everywhere (including on your organization's Web site). Next, take time at meetings or during lunch or coffee breaks to salute workers whose contributions underline that motivating phrase.

SIX: Reinforce specific work anniversaries or traditionally celebrated personal holidays by sending out handwritten messages wherever appropriate. Art Fry's Post-it® Notes (see Chapter Four) can be a great tool here. Try sticking a heartfelt compliment on an absent co-worker's computer screen and watch his or her eyes light up: *Congratulations on your three months with XYZ Company.* For even more fun – and more helpful recognition – try creating a note-based treasure hunt. Write out Post-its that contain directions and clues. When the treasure-hunters finally reach their goal (a festively decorated conference room?), bowl them over with a gaudy display of the public recognition they so richly deserve.

SEVEN: Score some recognition points with your top employees. Develop an internal points-based program that allows managers and other leadership figures to award company points or "bucks" when employees achieve specific goals that support the direction of the organization. Set it up so that these points can later be redeemed for various company-emblazoned awards and gifts.

EIGHT: Go public with your informal recognition as often as possible. Leverage the many different communication channels your organization uses to spread the message of achievement among all team members. Use the Internet and Intranet sites, company newsletters, letters mailed to the home, e-mail blasts, posters in the break-room and other high-visibility communications tools to maximize the effect.

NINE: Create some internal competition among departments by developing brief, objective-based contests that require meeting some new organizational goals. In most cases, your people will thoroughly enjoy competing for the bragging rights that usually flow from these kinds of high-spirited showdowns.

TEN: Make managers accountable for the recognition they give to their people. Keep in mind that more and more companies are using employee engagement and recognition as key criteria in determining how well managers are performing in their jobs.

CHAPTER NINE

Day-To-Day Recognition – Achieving the Daily *WOW!*

The Bottom Line: The latest research shows clearly that day-to-day recognition is a vitally important component in building a culture in which employees feel valued and appreciated. And the good news for managers and HR administrators everywhere is that it is not as complicated as one might think. According to one of America's bestselling business writers, in fact, "keeping it down-to-earth and simple" can do wonders for your emerging recognition program. Here's how to win big by keeping it simple.

Taking a Lesson from the Gridiron
There goes the football . . . 25 yards down the field . . . *Nice catch!*

It happens almost every weekday at a small manufacturing facility in Mentor, Ohio, where a very creative manager recently came up with a strikingly simple and powerfully effective way to encourage day-to-day recognition.

Invented on the spur of the moment by the thoughtful employee supervisor, the *Nice Catch!* program is wonderfully uncomplicated. It starts when a worker spots one of his or her colleagues making a contribution to the company's shared mission by coming up with a creative suggestion for the assembly line, let's say, or maybe hitting upon a clever solution to a packaging problem.

As soon as the observant employee notices the contribution, the day-to-day recognition scenario is set in motion, as follows:

First step: the observer grabs one of the dozen or so *Nice Catch!* new footballs that are stationed at various points around the facility.

Second step: The observer tosses the ball to the recipient, usually in front of several co-workers, while enthusiastically announcing to the group, "Nice catch, Joe! (or Susan, or Fred). You just earned a spot on the company football with your great solution to that problem."

Third step: Like a top NFL player, Joe autographs the ball.

From this point on, of course, the football is in play, and Joe becomes the current quarterback who must find the next receiver for the *Nice Catch!* award, by spotting a colleague who is performing at a high level. The current honoree will toss the ball to the new player, who will add his or her signature alongside the names of past hall-of-famers who have been recognized in the same fashion. When the ball is completely covered with signatures, it goes immediately to a large glass trophy case located just inside the front door of the facility as a way of honoring dozens of different workers for their daily contributions to their organization's mission.

Pretty simple, huh?

You bet it is. But if you're tempted to think that such uncomplicated, down-to-earth, daily recognition strategies are too simple to have a powerful impact on workers, think again.

According to renowned workplace analyst Patrick Lencioni, a bestselling author and consultant to numerous Fortune 500 corporations, creative recognition strategies like *Nice Catch!* are effective precisely because of their common sense simplicity. He says, "I've written half a dozen books on the psychology of the workplace, and if they've often found an enthusiastic audience, I think it's because I'm not afraid to be simple.

"Luckily for me, I'm not too intelligent for my own good. And if you think about it, what really counts when it comes to effective employee recognition programs is the ability to keep it simple and keep it real. Having the courage to embrace the simplest things and to avoid being distracted by the latest psychological gimmicks, that's one of the signs of a great organization in my view.

"I've done hundreds of interviews with organizational managers and employees alike over the years, and one of the themes that really stands out is that the best companies in the world aren't the ones with the most Ph.D.s. The best companies are the ones that understand such basic, universal concepts as 'love thy neighbor,' and then do their best to live up to those concepts every single day."

Lencioni can quickly tick off a few of the winners from his long list of success stories, a list that includes outfits like Southwest Airlines ("They treat their people like royalty – and their people respond.") and the restaurant chain Chick-fil-A ("They've put together one of the most enlightened employee recognition programs in the country, and everyone in their business knows it.").

Like Lencioni, most workplace analysts today regard the fast-growing Chick-fil-A as setting the gold standard in employee retention and loyalty. With a turnover among store operators of just 5 percent (compared to an industry average of 35 percent), this chain's tremendous success is thanks in large part to a broad-based recognition program that includes attractive awards for worker productivity and longevity, quick internal promotions and even a scholarship program for high-achieving employees who are also excelling in college.

The keys to making day-to-day recognition work, according to Lencioni, the San Francisco-based author of management bestsellers like *Death by Meeting* and *The Three Signs of a Miserable Job*, include such basic and uncomplicated qualities as honesty, open-mindedness and common sense – not to mention a keen sense of appreciation and awareness of everyone who works in your organization.

"These days, I don't think there's any question that the workplace has been going through some major changes," Lencioni explains. "For one thing, it's becoming clear that the retention of valued employees is probably more important now than it has ever been before.

"With the arrival of 'Generation Y' in the workplace, we're suddenly in a world in which the loyalty to a company isn't what it used to be. Let's face it; this isn't the same economy my dad knew, the kind of economy in which he was happy to work for 40 years for the same company. Today, workers tend to stay at a company for a few years, and then they want to move on. They want to become free agents, and you have to think long and hard about giving them a reason to stay."

Since today's employees are accustomed to frequent transition in their careers, the longevity of a 10-year employee is now on par with what a 25-year milestone represented just a few years ago. It's no wonder that most businesses can't afford to wait for an employee's five- or ten-year anniversary to acknowledge him or her for contributions to the organization. Businesses have found that if they don't significantly recognize employees early on, many of their best people won't stay engaged, and may quickly begin to look for new opportunities. Many business leaders make it a point to ensure that their new employees are recognized in a meaningful way on day one, at six months, on the first-year anniversary and many times in-between.

The North American workplace has been undergoing a sea of change during the past decade or so, and employee retention has become one of the major issues for managers. So how do you retain your best people through time? Giving them additional compensation won't do it, and giving them fancy titles or bigger offices won't work either.

What's needed is to create the kind of workplace environment that, with carefully thought-out strategies such as effective recognition programs, will make these talented folks feel right at home and where they will want to remain throughout their careers. If you get that element right, you'll be well on your way to building an organizational culture in which your key employees will continue to make vital contributions far into the future.

Day-To-Day Recognition: It's Infectious

OK. So far, so good. With Lencioni's lesson about the virtues of simplicity clearly in mind, let's turn now to the key question for all those who hope to improve their organizations by implementing or expanding effective recognition programs.

What's the best way to build day-to-day recognition?

The answers, of course, will be as varied and as creative as the thousands of business leaders and HR administrators who ask themselves each day how they can communicate better with their co-workers.

Among the many answers I've come up with working with businesses all around the world, a few general themes and recommendations seem to emerge again and again. They include the following:

---Managers need to train themselves to become praise professionals. During a recent recognition seminar that I led in Falls Church, Virginia, I was struck by a local bank HR director's gloomy description of her daily recognition experience. Her comment was, "The only time I'm ever recognized by my boss, the CFO, is if I spend too much money." Building a productive working relationship requires that managers take the time to notice when employees are doing things right instead of just when things go wrong. In fact, the best managers praise twice for every constructive criticism they offer.

---Instead of waiting to learn about major employee contributions, managers need to become proactive and spend part of each working day searching out employees' contributions that they can then reward on the spot. A great example happened during a very interesting experiment at a hospital in Amarillo, Texas, that armed managers and supervisors with "instant-recognition coupons" that are good for snacks and treats in the hospital cafeteria. The program has been a smash hit because it created the opportunity for instant recognition.

---Give managers tools that will help them effectively recognize their team members. A North Dakota technology company, for example, outfits each manager with a special recognition toolbox that contains a cornucopia of small but thoughtful gifts such as prepaid gas cards, T-shirts, company pins, and candy. The real driver behind the success of this program is that company policy requires every manager to empty his or her toolbox by the end of each month. When gifts are left over, managers need to justify why they couldn't find positives to reinforce.

---By encouraging other co-workers to applaud and recognize helpful contributions (as in the *Nice Catch!* scenario described above), managers can increasingly develop their own awareness of other workers and their daily efforts. The great thing about daily recognition in any organization is that it's infectious.

Once you begin to make this cultural change, it tends to be self-reinforcing and to take off on its own. And you'll then find that the people around you are also beginning to wake up to the realization that recognizing others simply makes life better for everyone involved in your enterprise – whether we're talking about the CEO or the guy mopping the floors at night.

Day-To-Day Recognition: Lucky Seven

It's a well-established fact; once your efforts at building a recognition culture reach critical mass, just about everybody in your organization will start to pick up on the positive vibes.

And once that happens, you'll begin to see some substantial changes in the way your workers, supervisors, and executive managers treat each other on the job.

Slowly, almost imperceptibly at first – but then with growing force and conviction – they'll begin to engage in the highly creative and constructive behavioral phenomenon known as day-to-day recognition.

The good news about this form of recognition, of course, is that it's extremely contagious! As many group-psychology studies have shown, recognition behavior is self-reinforcing, which means that it tends to inspire everyone who has been touched by it to become more and more aware of those around them. The best news is that everyone becomes increasingly motivated to contribute to the shared organizational mission.

Day-to-day recognition is a vitally important component in developing an overall culture of recognition that can change the way your people see themselves and each other.

Here are seven proven strategies aimed at helping all of us to better recognize each other's efforts every single day.

ONE: Keep employees in the loop. Studies show that a sense of being "in on things" is a top motivator for workers.   Every good manager knows that it's important to encourage feedback and input from the workers who report to them, but don't overlook the importance of keeping your people updated as well. Take note of groups and individuals who have had a hand in important projects, and ensure that those people are kept apprised of the project's progress and outcomes along the way. If Dana in the software group worked on a demo website for an important proposal, give her a report after the meeting with the client to let her know how it went -- good news or bad. This feedback loop is essential to grow and improve as a team. Good feedback will serve to bolster esteem and will give Dana an understanding of how her role contributed to the success of the endeavor. And if the outcome didn't meet expectations, that information will offer an important lesson for how the group can do better next time.

TWO: Open your staff or departmental meetings with a *WOW!* moment. Arrange in advance for one or two of your people to salute co-workers for their recent accomplishments at the beginning of your meeting. As you'll soon discover, the goodwill generated by this kind of peer-praise is infectious. If you can't find someone to open the meeting with a positive remark, then lead by example. Put together some upbeat recognition comments about two or three workers and do the job yourself.

THREE: Take advantage of the power contained in the English language – especially when it's written out by hand. Promise yourself that you'll send at least one handwritten note of praise every week. If that schedule sounds too ambitious, try once every two weeks until you get the hang of it. Here's where you can leverage office technology by entering these recognition tasks into your calendar as recurring appointments, along with lots of helpful information about the employees you want to honor in the weeks and months ahead.

FOUR: Never eat lunch alone. Whether you're planning to microwave last night's leftover lasagna in the lunchroom or are heading to the sub shop for the smoked turkey special, take an associate (or several) along for the meal. Lunch is a great time to connect with co-workers in a relaxed setting. Don't ever miss this chance to get to know your people on a new and different level.

FIVE: Ask your people for their opinions on work-related matters at least once a day and then make a continuous effort to praise their input later. It goes like this: "Bill, we finally decided to change the distribution process on that Colorado project. Your recommendations were very helpful in figuring it all out. Thanks for the great advice."

SIX: Create opportunities for accidental interactions with your people. Top industrial designers are structuring today's office interiors precisely to provide opportunities for colleagues to interact accidentally, and progressive employers have embraced this approach for creating a collaborative workplace setting. Some of the most insightful conversations and brilliant ideas come about during chance meetings in the hallway. Look for creative ways to encourage those spontaneous connections and don't forget to use these informal, unstructured conversations to recognize and praise your people for their outstanding work.

SEVEN: Frequently remind everyone (including yourself) of the link between their daily efforts and your organization's mission. If the purchasing department has negotiated a strategic partnership with a key vendor, praise them for it, but put that praise in a note that says something like, "Thanks for your diligence in working to set up our new relationship with OrangeWorks. This will be a tremendous asset in helping us succeed at our mission of becoming the most efficient and trusted supplier of citrus products in all of Florida."

CHAPTER TEN

Special Strategies for Achieving Retention

The Bottom Line: As survey after survey has shown, keeping your best people on the payroll throughout their productive years is crucial for your success as an organization. And the converse is also true; these days, the cost of retraining highly skilled employees to replace workers who leave can easily cut into profits. In this chapter, you'll meet a group of experts in employee retention who built one of the world's great retailing enterprises by figuring out how to use recognition strategies to keep their best people onboard.

Welcome to the Best Supermarket in the World

The Setting: A modern-day supermarket in the city of Rochester, New York.

The Scenario: A time-pressed food shopper is in search of some savory, imported blue cheese for her husband's fast-approaching retirement party.

Smiling expectantly, the loyal customer approached the counter in the huge deli section of her local supermarket.

Unlike so many 21st century American shoppers, this shopper didn't take a number and step off to the side to wait for service.

Instead of being forced to wait for help, she was pleased to see a smiling and enthusiastic employee in a bright blue apron instantly striding forward to meet her. "Good afternoon, Mrs. Burton, and welcome to Wegmans Food Markets. How can I help you today?"

Encouraged by the quick service, the customer cheerfully asked the clerk, "I'm hosting a retirement party for my husband, and I was hoping to pick up some imported blue cheese to go with the wine. You know, something really good? This is a very special occasion."

Nodding, the clerk smiled back at her. "You bet," he said energetically. "We carry more than 500 different cheeses and the blues are among our most popular varieties. Do you want to step this way?"

What followed was a highly successful moment in food-retailing, to say the least. While the customer listened attentively, the cheese clerk explained how blue cheese is manufactured, ending with the offer of half a dozen exquisitely flavorful samples (Gorgonzola, Roquefort, Stilton, and others) from several different regions of Europe.

For the delighted cheese-seeker, of course, it was another great example of why she had become a loyal Wegmans customer forever.

For the legendary Wegmans Food Markets, that moment of outstanding service at the deli was a strictly routine occurrence. Not surprising, since the supermarket was described by food analyst Neil Stern, quoted in a front page story of the *Wall Street Journal,* as "the best supermarket chain in the country, and maybe in the world."

The extremely pleased customer did not know that the Olde

World cheese clerk who helped her that day had spent more than 40 hours in a training program (known as 'Cheese University'), from which every new Wegmans employee working in the cheese department is required to graduate.

In order to create Wegmans, which now operates 71 stores in New York, Pennsylvania, New Jersey, Virginia and Maryland, some of the smartest trailblazers in the food industry had put their heads together and come up with a simple but powerfully effective philosophy: Meet the needs of your employees and they, in turn, will take care of your customers.

Having settled on this powerful theme, the Wegmans' brass set about figuring out how to create fabulous customer service. What CEO Danny Wegman and his merchandising lieutenants soon realized was that exquisitely good service requires employees who are truly dedicated to providing it. With that in mind, Wegmans developed employee training and recognition programs that are second to none. At Wegmans, which now employs more than 37,000 workers, employees are reminded constantly that they are greatly valued and respected by their management.

To build its loyal and skilled workforce, Wegmans begins its program of employee appreciation and recognition with the basics. Like most effective managers, the leaders at Wegmans acknowledge the importance of providing their people with highly competitive compensation and benefits.

But to distance itself from the pack in its marketplace, Wegmans begins with a remarkably comprehensive training program that covers every aspect of the food industry in the 21st century. The Wegmans quest for knowledge also extends to general education. At this enlightened company, both full-time and part-time employees are eligible to receive college scholarship help from the company -

yet another way the firm continues to set the national standard for valuing and recognizing its employees.

The company is obviously doing something right; its employee turnover rate now stands at less than 6 percent compared to nearly 20 percent for the food industry as a whole.

It's also why *FORTUNE* magazine has put Wegmans in the top three best companies to work for every year since the listing began in 1998; in fact, in 2005, Wegmans was ranked number one on the list.

Throughout the entire Wegmans operation, the emphasis on providing better service by respecting and recognizing employees is the order of the day. On the first morning of new employee orientation (known as "Welcome to Wegmans Day") at corporate headquarters in Rochester, President Danny Wegman shows up bright and early and then personally delivers a detailed presentation that introduces the newcomers to the operation.

In a recent *Buffalo News* article, Lynne Moore, a long-time HR manager at the wildly successful chain, summed it up nicely: "When your employees are happy and they feel like they're taken care of, they're going to take care of the customers."

Win the Battle for Employee Retention: Here's How

So how successful has this extraordinary supermarket enterprise been at that most crucial of management tasks – employee retention?

At Wegmans, the numbers speak for themselves; more than 20 percent of the company's workforce has been on the job for more than a decade. Even more amazing in an industry that's notorious for rapid turnover is the fact that Wegmans has more than 1,000 employees who can claim at least 25 years of service. And all 1,000 consistently show up for work, eager to provide more of their world-famous service to customers.

In an era when the cost of replacing quality employees can easily reach 50 percent of an employee's compensation package, there's no doubt that retaining top people must be the first and most essential task of effective managers and HR administrators. Keeping your best employees onboard isn't just a frill, it's an absolute necessity in an age when the fiercely competitive global marketplace increasingly rewards enterprises that are wise enough (and disciplined enough) to maintain their high-tech and frequently specialized employees on the payroll.

As the Wegmans employee recognition program makes clear, organizations that know how to recognize their workers – through structured formal recognition and more casual informal presentations (and also via those on-the-spot moments of recognition that can happen over a cup of coffee) – will be perfectly positioned to win the battle for employee retention and, as a result, to enjoy the ample benefits that follow.

Wegmans' leadership embraces many of the strategies detailed in this book, beginning with its tradition of honoring employees' service with yearly formal events to recognize staffers who are reaching significant anniversaries. Rounding out its formal program, Wegmans reinforces its business mission through significant awards for customer service excellence. The results of these two formal initiatives are plain: exceptional employee retention and exceptionally happy customers.

Wegmans' recognition program also includes a widely varied array of informal activities for staffers, including everything from yearly company picnics to company-sponsored softball and basketball teams in local recreational leagues to exciting presentations at local high schools where students who work part-time at Wegmans are awarded scholarships for college. These kinds of social events serve to build community and enhance workplace relationships.

These are powerful incentives, of course, and, taken together, have helped Wegmans to achieve one of the best employee retention rates in the industry.

Wegmans' analysts and managers will also tell you that the company's approach to retention is also strongly supported by its day-to-day recognition program, in which supermarket managers and department heads throughout the entire 71-store chain constantly walk the aisles and talk with staffers about ways to improve the company's legendary service.

At Wegmans, one of the keys to success is a philosophy that encourages managers not to sit in their offices studying balance sheets or inventories all day long. At these supermarkets, managers are constantly on the move, and everywhere they go, they're talking with the employees, praising them and encouraging them to do an even better job of putting the customer first.

As many food industry analysts have pointed out, Wegmans is an all-star in combining formal, informal and day-to-day recognition in a carefully thought-out approach to employee retention. Its results prove beyond a reasonable doubt that such recognition is a vital tool in keeping your best people on the job and keeping satisfied customers coming through the doors.

Boosting Retention Through Recognition:
A Primer

Quiz time! Got your pencil? To test your knowledge, circle the correct answer to the following question.

How much does employee turnover cost American business each year, according to the U.S. Department of Labor?

> A. $100 billion
> B. $500 billion
> C. $900 billion
> D. $5 trillion

If you circled "D," you're well on your way to grasping the key point of this chapter: the fact that loss of key employees to turnover is by far the largest single unplanned expense in business today.

Employee turnover is a huge headache for everyone involved, of course. But why let it swamp your organization in needless red ink? As business leaders have been discovering, effective recognition strategies can keep employee turnover at bay.

Here's an employee retention primer designed to help you do just that.

ONE: Start retaining on day 1 – The first week of a new job is an extremely impressionable time, and it represents an important opportunity to build a productive and fulfilling relationship between the new employee and the business. At Founders Bank & Trust in the Midwest, President Laurie Beard personally meets with every new employee and presents him or her with a Welcome Aboard award, a silver Founders pin that includes their corporate symbol. Founders Bank & Trust is highly selective in the hiring process, and only the best are presented with an offer to join the proud team. According to Laurie, recognizing the beginning of a Founders Bank & Trust career builds a foundation for a productive future.

TWO: Remember that one of the best and most motivating forms of recognition you can provide to co-workers is your continuing confidence in their ability to meet new challenges. Dare to believe in them fully and keep raising the bar by coming up with new assignments that test their skills and their creativity. If you can help to make their careers challenging and rewarding, you'll greatly increase the odds that they'll remain with your organization.

THREE: Try to include co-workers' significant others in recognition events and other important career moments, whenever possible. By making sure that a spouse and/or other close family members of your valued employee are connected with your organization, you'll be sending a powerful message. That message reads, "We value you and your family, and we want to keep you with us."

FOUR: Keep asking your people about their goals and aspirations. How can you know what will motivate and inspire them if you don't ask? From time to time, take a valued employee to lunch and use the time to pose several key questions. What do you like most about your job? What is your most exciting and thrilling challenge? If you could go anywhere you wanted in this organization, where would it be? If you stay ahead of the motivational curve with your workers, you should be able to anticipate their needs, an important step in providing them with the career advancement opportunities that will keep them in your organization.

FIVE: Encourage and reward career growth. Support your employees' desires to acquire new skill sets and don't miss the opportunity to acknowledge those achievements. A more highly trained workforce stands a better chance of succeeding in the global marketplace. Frequently, companies develop awards that offer visible symbols of successfully learned skills to recognize employees' educational achievements. Consider how a diploma becomes a source of pride for the new graduate or how a nurse proudly wears an RN pin. In the same way, those who "graduate" to a new level in your organization will treasure an award that commemorates reaching a new level in their training.

SIX: Blow the trumpet for your people. Getting the word out about successful workers and their accomplishments can support employee retention. Frequently, local newspapers and business journals are looking for employee success and achievement stories. Don't hesitate to contact these media outlets as a way to get the message out. Imagine how proud your employees will feel about their achievements and their workplace when a neighbor or buddy comments about seeing their accomplishments highlighted in the business section of the newspaper.

SEVEN: Find interesting and entertaining new ways of saying thanks for a job well done, and make sure everybody in your organization gets to participate in the recognition experience. In North Andover, Massachusetts, the HR professionals who work at a large retirement community recently came up with a fun recognition game based on bingo. In this variation of the popular game, the HR managers wait until one of their employee teams reaches a production or service goal, and then they reward the entire staff by launching a day-long bingo game. During the course of the workday, bingo numbers are announced over the intercom. As the enthused employees mark their cards, the team that reached the productivity goal is being recognized again and again for its outstanding accomplishment. Winners take home prizes and the workers who made it all possible continue to bask in the radiant spotlight of employee recognition.

EIGHT: You get what you reward. Want your employees to stay with your organization? Show them that their service is valued and appreciated by recognizing it. There is a reason that recognition for length of service continues to be the foundation of virtually every recognition program in North American business. Successful organizations build employee relationships that are fulfilling for their people and for the business. Like any relationship, celebrating significant milestones is important.

CHAPTER ELEVEN

Special Strategies for Achieving Improved Production and Customer Satisfaction

The Bottom Line: In this book about strategies for creating and continually expanding the *WOW!* **Workplace**, we've laid out the concepts that will help you build a culture of recognition within your organization. But how can you target that recognition in order to achieve the crucially important twin goals of increased production and enhanced customer satisfaction? You'll find many of the answers to that key question in the following story about a start-up company that went from zero annual revenues to more than $6 billion within the space of five years.

Behind the Scenes at the Birth of Google

One mild spring morning a few years ago, a 41-year-old marketing executive arrived for her first day of work at a startup Internet services company located in a suburb of San Francisco, California.

Her name was Cindy McCaffrey and she was about to start her

first day as the director of corporate communications at a brand-new business enterprise that few people had ever heard of.

The name of that fledgling enterprise was *Google.*

McCaffrey was enthused about the creative challenge, and she became even more enthused when she saw how the new company (the brainchild of two extraordinarily gifted Internet entrepreneurs who were also former grad students from nearby Stanford University) was treating its employees.

In those early days at Google, the two engineering wizards who had founded the company (Larry Page and Sergey Brin) were still in their late 20s. Armed with a paradigm-changing Internet search algorithm that would allow its users to instantly pinpoint information on the Net, the wizards were also determined to create a new kind of company that would be built around a dramatically new approach to employee recognition – though they didn't even know it at the time.

Now, as McCaffrey hurried through the maze of engineering labs and computer-cluster workstations that formed the heart of the startup, she was getting her first look at their new approach.

Her first eyebrow-raising observation was that several employees had brought their dogs to work. Then what about all those brightly colored exercise balls that the newly hired computer engineers and software code-writers were alternately using as chairs or tossing back and forth in the hallways and work spaces?

And what about their attire? As McCaffrey later recounted, there were approximately 30 staffers on the job that day (they were among Google's first hires) and not one of them, male or female, was clad in traditional business attire. Instead, most of these dog-loving and ball-tossing employees wore torn jeans, colorful tank tops and flip-flops.

Looking back on her first morning in the Palo Alto offices of Google, McCaffrey remembers briefly wondering if "these two guys were really serious about starting a new business and trying to grow it from scratch."

But her doubts soon evaporated as the Google enterprise quickly took off. Within the next five years or so, the newly launched company would morph at mach speed from a shoestring operation in a converted backyard garage into a $6 billion-a-year behemoth that became a household brandname in every corner of the world.

McCaffrey is often credited with playing a major role in the Google success story by designing its immensely effective marketing strategy from the get-go. She says the key to the new company's sudden takeoff could be found in the "creative energy and willingness to challenge assumptions," which was the concept that had motivated the two entrepreneurs from the very beginning.

"These two guys were determined to find new ways to use information technology to make the world a better place," says McCaffrey today. "And they challenged every single thing you told them. They made you think about the way you had been doing things.

"Working at Google during its first few years was an exciting, exhilarating experience. And I think all of us who worked there could tell that we were involved in something very special – the birth of a new vision of how technology could be used to help people all around the globe, and a new vision of how to create and sustain a new company by recruiting all sorts of talented, creative, vibrant people."

McCaffrey also credits the super-talented Page and Brin with embracing the concept of employee recognition by creating a corporate culture in which the people who worked at the startup company were simply regarded as the friends and family of the owners. At the same time, all employees were being encouraged to tap into their creativity in order to solve the immensely complicated problems that were part of creating a major international communications company in little more than half a decade.

One of the most important things the new company did was to focus a tremendous amount of energy on giving each of its employees the sense of a shared stake in the company's success – both financially and emotionally. Energized by the realization that they were working toward something important, the people who labored at the startup during the early years were totally motivated to bring their creative best to the workplace each day.

From the very beginning, Google started a foundation for their unique culture using all the standard tools of employee recognition, including length-of-service awards and awards for special contributions to its corporate mission, along with spontaneous, day-to-day recognition of workers who came up with new wrinkles in marketing and computer engineering. But the visionary startup went far beyond these standard recognition practices to build a **WOW! Workplace** that soon became a model of employee recognition for organizations worldwide.

Describing how this powerfully effective culture of recognition dramatically boosted production and creative problem-solving during the early days of Google, McCaffrey points to the wildly successful corporation's official philosophy, which it has named *Ten Things Google Has Found To Be True*.

Number nine in that list says,

"Google's founders have often stated that the company is not serious about anything but search. They built a company around the idea that work should be challenging and the challenge should be fun. To that end, Google's culture is unlike any in corporate America, and it's not because of the ubiquitous lava lamps and large rubber balls, or the fact that the company's chef used to cook for the Grateful Dead.

In the same way Google puts users first when it comes to our online service, Google Inc. puts employees first when it comes to daily life in our Googleplex headquarters. There is an emphasis on team achievements and pride in individual accomplishments that contributes to the company's overall success. Ideas are traded, tested and put into practice with an alacrity that can be dizzying. Meetings that would take hours elsewhere are frequently little more than a conversation in line for lunch and few walls separate those who write the code from those who write the checks.

This highly communicative environment fosters a productivity and camaraderie fueled by the realization that millions of people rely on Google results. Give the proper tools to a group of people who like to make a difference, and they will."

A Key Lesson from Google: Listen to the Janitor

There's no question that the Google startup saga now looms as one of the great stories in the history of modern business.

Reading that story, many of us who work daily to improve communication and the recognition of workers at organizations large and small will come away with a deeply challenging question: How can we use the "Lessons of Google" to enhance our own productivity and, in many cases, to improve that all-important commodity known as customer satisfaction?

The answers to that question, it seems, are as varied as the organizations and the companies we each strive to build every day.

Still, if you look at how the Google geniuses put together their remarkable enterprise in only a few years, a few basic themes do seem to come clear. Among those themes are several that lie at the heart of **The *WOW!* Workplace**, including:

---***Recognizing the creativity*** of workers in an open-minded, enthusiastic, and always honest way is absolutely essential for creating the kind of recognition culture that will allow your organization to flourish.

---***Challenging your assumptions*** about workers and your daily relationship with those same workers can pay handsome dividends. In what ways can your organization become more flexible and more creative in its day-to-day dealings with the people who make it successful?

---***Most important of all***, perhaps, is the willingness to trust your people to come up with the solutions and suggestions your organization needs most in order to prosper and flourish. Remember the story of the janitor in California who questioned the need to tear up 20 floors of a big hotel in order to install a new elevator? Remember how his simple, amazingly helpful suggestion ("Install the elevator outside the building") wound up saving that business more than $1 million?

If there's a single recognition lesson for all of us in the great story of how Google built a business empire in the wink of an eye, it's probably this:

Listen carefully to everybody in your organization, and listen all the time; be sure to include the janitors.

Enhancing Productivity Via Recognition: Eight Hot Tips

Take a stroll through the busy offices of a high-tech e-commerce services company in Port Arthur, Texas, and the odds are high that you'll observe a boisterous ritual taking place.

At the bustling communications facility in this southeast Texas city, employees and managers long ago became accustomed to frequent announcements on the company's strategically placed intercom system:

"Congratulations to Bill Smith in Software Quality Control. Thanks to your very helpful creative suggestion this morning, you've just won a Reward Buck."

At this technology company, where managers often hand out specially designed "dollar bills" that work in all onsite snack and drink machines, the periodic presentation of Reward Bucks is an important part of the firm's widely praised and highly creative, on-the-spot employee recognition program.

And guess what? Since implementing the Reward Bucks system (along with several other innovative programs aimed at boosting output), the company has seen steady increases in productivity throughout all of its Port Arthur-based computer operations.

How can your organization use this kind of "recognition magic" to improve both on-the-job productivity and customer service? Here are eight strategies aimed at inspiring the people who can make it happen: your co-workers.

ONE: Start recognizing your people in the present tense. Numerous psychological studies show that the longer you wait to acknowledge an employee's contribution to your mission, the less impact your recognition will have. The real power of the Reward Bucks is in their immediacy, for example. Most people tend to respond with lots of energy in situations where the reward for accomplishments takes place almost instantly.

TWO: Join the club. Develop an exclusive club or elite group within your organization based on meeting productivity goals. Induct members into your "Circle of Excellence" or "Chairman's Club" who have attained a specific level of success for the business. Like most recognition initiatives, there are no cast-in-stone parameters to this group. It changes from business to business, but it should be aligned with your organizational goals. It's important to set the bar at a level that challenges without being out of reach. Most programs are open to everyone who can hit a specific number or metric. The more winners, the better.

THREE: Develop a recognition committee. Get other recognition activists involved in the process of developing your recognition culture. Assign your crusaders the task of helping to identify areas within your organization where recognition is being neglected and brainstorm creative ways to recognize those employees. I've worked with many businesses in which recognition committees have been able to greatly enhance the informal and day-to-day recognition experience of their employees. Certainly, committees need leadership who will ensure that the proposed schemes help the business appropriately reach its goals.

FOUR: Business storytelling is a resurgent trend. Even as our world progresses technologically, the age-old art of business storytelling is increasingly becoming an important communication tool. The practice of sharing stories about the company's past, its people and its purpose is an interactive tool organizational leaders use to enable their employees to connect emotionally with the company's goals, learn from history, and have a greater understanding about what can be achieved. This trend is a powerful way to encompass employee engagement and recognition when it highlights individual and group achievements to encourage others to emulate those behaviors.

FIVE: Market your recognition program to your employees. Want your employees to get fired up about their opportunities to be recognized at work? Tell them about it! More than once. The mantra in advertising is 'repetition, repetition, repetition.' In order for a recognition program to motivate a group, workers need to understand why the program is in place, what it is meant to accomplish, and how employees are impacted by their achievements. With a little creativity, the options are endless. A couple of ideas: send out monthly e-mails to the whole workgroup that congratulate people who are on course to meet their productivity goals. Use posters in your breakrooms that show pictures of the different awards employees can earn for their achievements. Post your mission statement on your company Intranet site and a link that shows how the organization recognizes its people for contributing to the mission.

SIX: Include a highly productive employee in new-hire interviews during which you explain to the applicant, "I've asked Bill Smith to join us because he has a great track-record in the area where you'll be working. He has really helped to increase our productivity. I thought it would be helpful for him to tell you about our productivity goals." (This is one of those nice management moments when you get two for the price of one. Bill gets a nice pat on the back and the new hire now knows that you expect productivity goals to be met or even surpassed.)

SEVEN: Take time to celebrate. Many companies highlight a specific day or week during which to celebrate individual, team, and companywide achievements. The traditions of Employee Appreciation Day, Engineering Week, Customer Service Day, and so forth, can be powerful productivity boosters when they provide an opportunity for team members to reflect on their accomplishments and get a fresh perspective on their future goals. Frequently, these celebrations include various fun events like bocce on the front lawn or an annual chili cook-off, activities that also encourage and support company togetherness. The festivities often culminate in a formal presentation of significant awards, leaving employees energized, focused, and positioned to work together for success in the coming year.

EIGHT: Design your own on-the-spot system for providing recognition via thoughtful notes, treats or small gifts that can be handed out spontaneously. The possibilities are practically limitless in this area of employee recognition – provided you take the time to plan your awards so they work effectively and don't fall flat. While some managers keep a stack of free movie passes in their desks for such occasions, others prefer coupons for gallons of gas, or even free back-and-neck massages at the downtown health center. To figure out the on-the-spot program that will work most effectively for you, spend some time thinking about the personality of your workplace, and then design your strategy accordingly.

While giving a recognition seminar recently in west Texas, I heard a human resource professional describe an inexpensive approach to on-the-spot recognition that has worked well at a large construction company worksite. It goes like this: when a worker is consistently performing at a high level, the foreman will grab a two-by-four and secretly ask everybody on the crew to sign it. After the foreman writes out a thank-you salute on the board, the trophy is presented to the worker. According to the HR pro at this construction company, the inscribed boards have become treasured mementos among the workers who hang onto them for years.

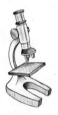

CHAPTER TWELVE

The Future Is Now

The Bottom Line: With more than 70 million members of the techno-savvy and highly mobile Generation-Y entering the U.S. workplace, there's no doubt that the challenges facing business leaders and HR administrators are becoming increasingly formidable. The good news is that those managers who have learned how to build a powerful culture of recognition are ideally positioned to adjust quickly to changing workplace conditions.

Arriving on the Scene: Generation-Y

Dr. Blake Hill's state-of-the-art structural biology lab at the world-renowned Johns Hopkins University in Baltimore is an amazing sight to see...and it starts with the T-shirts.

On a typical weekday morning at Dr. Hill's Intracellular Communications Networks Laboratory, which is the setting for some of the most exciting research on protein structure being performed today, you're likely to find four or five young investigators working hard at their microscopes. It would be difficult not to notice that they are clad in bright-blue T-shirts that communicate the lighthearted slogan: TEAM PROTEIN.

You'll also notice that their boss (one of the world's leading researchers on the biochemical mechanisms that underlie such diseases as cancer and diabetes) is proudly wearing his own hand-crafted shirt – a shapeless, well-worn garment that features the slogan: *The Usual Suspects: Under Investigation By The Biology Department.* Beneath the words is a series of colorfully drawn cartoons of the creatures (a C. elegans worm, a Drosophila fruit fly, a grinning rat, and an impish-looking yeast particle) that laboratory biologists typically use in conducting their research.

At first glance, the presence of so much devil-may-care informality in one of the nation's most cutting-edge disease labs might seem surprising. But if you ask Dr. Hill for an explanation, he quickly points out that it's actually quite appropriate.

"We work very hard in this lab, and we're usually up until all hours of the night chasing molecules," says the balding, 45-year-old scientist. "But we also know how to relax and enjoy ourselves. And that's important, especially when you remember that most of our graduate researchers – the young people who actually staff this lab – are in their mid-20s. They were raised differently than we older folks, and there's no doubt that they come from a very different generation than the one I grew up in.

"These young people are the first wave of the next generation – the group some refer to as Generation-Y – and they have some very different ideas about what the workplace should be, and about what should go on there. They're far less structured than my generation was, and they don't look at the organizations they work for in the traditional, paternalistic way that so many of us did."

Adds Dr. Hill, explaining how the nation's 70 million Gen-Y-ers (they're also known as Millennials) are bringing major changes to the workplace, "I grew up in a world where many young people still hoped to find a good job and then stay with that company for the rest of their working lives. But this new generation is very different.

"They don't necessarily feel that same loyalty to their employers, and they're much more self-sufficient. They're also technically proficient since most have been using computers daily since they were children. All that interaction with technology has given them a sense of time that is different. These folks are accustomed to getting the things they want in a hurry, and you have to manage them with that thought in mind.

"They're also accustomed to challenging authority figures. They question absolutely everything. If you can't handle that kind of honest open-mindedness, you aren't going to be able to manage them very well."

Lora Picton, one of the youthful, T-shirt-wearing researchers in Dr. Hill's lab, says she couldn't agree more about the differences between his generation of scientists and her own. But she also says that Dr. Hill's recognition and acceptance of those differences – and his willingness to be flexible as a supervisor – is the key to his recent success in building one of this country's top biology research labs. "Dr. Hill knows how to laugh; that's for sure," says Picton. "He's also very generous in terms of letting us work on projects that we're especially interested in. He's enthusiastic and supportive – and that's very important when you're managing a team of researchers who are still in their 20s."

The 3 Most Important Steps on the Road to *WOW!*

Like Blake Hill in Baltimore, thousands of business leaders and HR professionals are beginning to feel the impact of Gen-Y on the workplace. As workplace demographics change, the typical job environment will be altered in ways that can't be fully predicted right now.

Still, a few Gen-Y trends are already beginning to make themselves known in the contemporary workplace; among these are the following:

---Workers will switch employers far more frequently than in the past. Millennials have an appetite for new and varied experiences; they have instant access to information about new opportunities; and, they don't have the same view of employers as paternalistic figures who deserve their permanent loyalty. Growing numbers of workplace observers are convinced that we're about to inherit a national workforce who consider a worker with five years of service to be a veteran employee. If that happens as predicted, managers are going to have to adjust their ideas about length-of-service recognition accordingly – and quickly. At the same time, it will become more and more important to encourage and reward training and advancement within our companies in order to satisfy our Gen-Y workers' unquenchable thirst for professional growth and new experiences.

---Workers will put more emphasis on whether the job gives them opportunities to use their creativity and their imaginations as opposed to traditional incentives like compensation, fringe benefits, competitive bonuses, and rapid promotions. Although these traditional incentives will still be important to some, Generation-Y doesn't value them as much as previous generations. Because the Millennials have played on soccer teams that gave every kid a trophy whether they won or lost, they have learned to expect recognition for their individual efforts and their group contributions. To motivate them will require a great deal of thought and ingenuity. Team-oriented recognition programs will be effective along with individual

recognition. Open-ended incentive programs, in which everyone who meets objectives is rewarded, will replace individual recognition programs like employee-of-the-month programs where only one person can earn the reward.

---*The Gen-Y workers value work-life balance* perhaps more than any previous generation. Because of the way communications have speeded up and become omnipresent (with the arrival of e-mail, cell phones linked to the Internet, BlackBerrys® and numerous other digital assistants), many employees can "go to work" from anywhere, at any time. In this 24/7 virtual environment, it's important for employees to carve out enough personal time in which to enjoy and experience a balanced life. Business leaders need to be sensitive to this change in the office environment. As it relates to effective recognition, more and more managers will be called upon to be receptive to work that gets done outside of the workplace -- whether it's an offsite employee or a worker who logs in from home to complete an assignment after "normal" hours. Noticing and recognizing these contributions that take place outside of work walls become increasingly important.

As a result, these changes in perspective will bring enormous challenges for all of us who work to help organizations become better by building powerfully effective cultures of recognition.

There may well be lots of change in the days ahead, but basic human nature probably won't change. Underlining that point, Society for Human Resource Management (SHRM) Chief Knowledge Officer Dr. Debra Cohen likes to point out, "I think it's important to remember that everybody thought the Baby Boomers were going to change the workplace forever.

"Remember how different some of the hippies and anti-war people seemed back in the 1960s? But the fact is that they grew and changed; they matured and, in the end, they turned out to be not all that different from their predecessors in the workplace. Sure, there will be changes in the years ahead, but we also have to remember that human nature does tend to remain pretty constant. I don't think we should overdo all of this Generation-Y stuff for that reason."

And of course it's also true that regardless of how complex the work environment or how fast the pace of life becomes, most people are still going to require authentic personal respect and appreciation for the tasks they're asked to complete each day.

They're also going to continue to need appropriate recognition – formal, informal and day-to-day – in order to perform at the levels of productivity that are required by global competition. As this book has attempted to point out on every page, such recognition has always been the linchpin that holds organizations together to accomplish their shared missions. No matter how complex and demanding the economic realities of our time may eventually become, history shows us that motivating the members of your organization by recognizing them will still lie at the heart of every organizational success.

In my years of research and travel to discuss the art of recognition with business and organizational leaders worldwide, I've listened to literally thousands of suggestions about ways to make sure you're motivating and inspiring your people to the max by honoring their efforts every single day. Again and again, however, the tips and suggestions I heard (and many are contained in this book) seemed to circle back to three basic concepts that lie at the very heart of recognition.

FIRST: Employees want to be recognized as unique individuals. We all want to be appreciated for the qualities that make each of us special. Business leaders are wise to respond to this need by considering how they can recognize their employees in a personal way to demonstrate that they value the individual person. When choosing awards for individuals, it's key to select awards that are exclusive and that show an understanding of the individual's achievements and contributions to the business.

SECOND: Employees value personal interactions and consistent feedback at work. Gen-Y has a strong affinity for social experiences that's paired with a voracious craving for feedback on their performance. But these needs are not unique to that age group. As managers, it becomes increasingly important to learn how to develop good people skills. Managers who learn to communicate appreciation for their people on a day-to-day basis, and who recognize significant milestones and achievements in a meaningful way, will be more successful at motivating and leading their people. Providing supervisors with effective training on how to recognize their people, as well as a structure for recognition, is vital to supporting them in accomplishing these goals.

THIRD: Employees are motivated to contribute to something greater than themselves. This is the piece that ties it all together as you work to build up both your business and your people. When developing your recognition program, remember that one of the most powerful experiences you can offer your employees is the chance to excel and to contribute to a shared mission. Be sure to recognize your people for the ways that they help your business succeed, and offer awards that symbolize the connection between the organization and the individuals who are contributing to its success.

As you have no doubt already surmised, these three concepts aren't unique to Generation-Y. These basic human principles apply to each of us as we work together to make our businesses better.

The future is now, and there's no better time to begin influencing the culture around you through effective recognition. Just like training for a triathlon, the first step is to take the first step.

If you follow the guides outlined in this book – and if you put your heart and soul into developing the kind of personal leadership that's required to build a culture of recognition – you'll be well positioned to create the kind of *WOW!* **Workplace** that will allow your organization to keep growing and prospering far into the future.

Recognizing Today's Younger Workers:
Eight Strategies

HR leaders and business people everywhere are confronting a formidable challenge: how to motivate and engage Gen- Y workers with recognition strategies best suited to their unique attitudes and expectations as employees.

Because Gen-Y grew up in a digital world and are long-accustomed to using instant messaging, online social networking, and browsing the Web for anything and everything, these youthful workers inhabit a psychological landscape that differs in some ways from that of previous generations.

Broadly speaking, Gen-Y workers expect instanta-

neous feedback in virtually everything they do. This generation is deeply social, and many Millennials are accustomed to
relationships in which they receive validation and affirmation
in their everyday pursuits, which means that managers are
probably going to have to be more attentive to their workers
than in the past.

Perhaps most importantly, business leaders need to learn
to respond to Gen-Y's different perspectives on their careers.
Highly mobile and highly experiential, this next generation of
workers is almost certain to trigger some important changes
in the formal, informal, and day-to-day recognition programs
taking place around them.

How can your organization best respond to these now-
unfolding changes in the workplace? Here are eight strategies
designed to help you better recognize Millennials.

ONE: Tie recognition awards and key recognition
moments to professional development. The latest research
shows clearly that Gen-Y members are highly goal-oriented.
They are wired to solving problems and then seeing the
results of their solutions in real time. HR leaders can connect
with this trend and make their recognition programs more
effective by linking awards and presentations to professional
development. For instance, to honor a group of IT employees
who made a special contribution to your organization, sign
them up for a free seminar in their area of expertise (such as
specialized programming or data-mining).

TWO: Give bragging rights. Tangible symbols
of accomplishment are arguably more important to Gen-
Y employees than they have been to other generations. A
physical award that a young high-achiever can display in his or

her workspace, or take home to show off to family members, will be highly motivational and a great confidence booster.

THREE: Make the recognition process part of assigning new responsibilities. Let's say you're taking two or three high-achieving Gen-Y workers to a special lunch in honor of their recent performance. For maximum impact with this group, which is often described as seeking "instant gratification," don't just serve up your praise along with the Caesar salad and the chicken croquettes. Instead, link your salutes to each with a new responsibility, as in: "Bill, in light of your recent contributions, which we're honoring here today, we're assigning you to help lead that new initiative aimed at growing our online marketing efforts."

FOUR: Include rewards that support work-life balance goals and flexibility as part of your recognition program. Many studies show that these issues are often more important to Gen-Y than compensation or fringe benefits. Consider ways that your award structure can support the extracurricular interests and social needs of your employees. Gen-Y employees, in particular, tend to respond in a highly positive way to recognition awards that allow them to choose an item for themselves that suits their hobbies or social interests. This is certainly why more and more employers are incorporating award-selection programs into their recognition packages that include such fun rewards as camping equipment, a cooler for the beach, luggage for travel or athletic equipment. As you consider lifestyle award options like these, keep in mind that all appropriate awards need to incorporate a symbolic tie into your business. To accomplish this, businesses integrate the company's emblem or corporate symbol into the award to serve as a reminder of the award's meaning.

FIVE: Create goal-oriented recognition criteria with short timespans and crystal-clear metrics. Research shows that Millennials are keenly interested in achieving goals rapidly, so managers need to devise recognition programs that allow for bite-sized measurements even if the rewards contain minimal monetary value. It could be as simple as setting aside 10 minutes every Friday afternoon at the same time to present these awards to the people who are meeting goals in your workplace.

SIX: Send kudos home. For many Gen-Y employees, parents and mentors play a significant role as these individuals grow into their early careers. Though it may surprise some business leaders, research with Millennial employees indicates that many of these folks appreciate messages that their employers send home to their parents that communicate approval for their on-the-job performance.

SEVEN: Make sure your recognition initiatives are online. Most Gen-Y employees don't recall a world without the Internet, and for that reason see it as a very personal medium for interaction. To ensure that your organization's recognition programs are connecting with this group, make sure that award selection options and internal program communications are available via this channel.

EIGHT: Embrace recognition strategies that leverage the technology that Gen-Y grew up with and uses on a daily basis. Broadcast text messages / w 2 g! u r gr8 ;-) / to your employee group's cell phones regarding team members' achievements and successes. This also ensures that the message is received on a timely basis. Take advantage of external online communication mechanisms for public acknowledgement. For example, post your praise as a comment on a deserving employee's Facebook or MySpace page for peers to see. Try starting a company recognition blog, host an internal webcast on recognition, or make podcasts available that highlight outstanding accomplishments. Consider using YouTube as a communication channel where you can upload tasteful videos to convey your business values or the details of your recognition program. In certain situations you may even post a video of your awards event. Using new tools is one way to keep your message fresh.